THE
LIBRARIAN'S
THESAURUS

by
Mary Ellen Soper
Larry N. Osborne
Douglas L. Zweizig

with the assistance of
Ronald R. Powell

edited by Mary Ellen Soper

AMERICAN LIBRARY ASSOCIATION

Chicago and London 1990

Designed by Michael Brierton

Composed by Point West, Inc., on a Compugraphic Quadex
5000 and output on a Compugraphic 8600 digital
typesetter in English Times, with Caslon and
Triumvirate

Printed on 50-pound Glatfelter, a pH-neutral stock,
and bound in 10-point Carolina cover stock by
Edwards Brothers, Inc.

The paper used in this publication meets the minimum requirements of American National
Standard for Information Sciences—Permanence of Paper for Printed Library Materials, ANSI
Z39.48-1984. ∞

Library of Congress Cataloging-in-Publication Data

Soper, Mary Ellen.
 The librarian's thesaurus : a concise guide to library and information terms / edited by Mary
Ellen Soper ; by Mary Ellen Soper, Larry N. Osborne, Douglas L. Zweizig.
  p. cm.
  ISBN 0-8389-0530-7 (alk. paper)
  1. Library science—Dictionaries. 2. Information science—Dictionaries. I. Osborne,
Larry N. II. Zweizig, Douglas. III. Title.
 Z1006.S595 1990
 020′.3—dc20   90-147

OUTLINE OF CONTENTS

FIGURES

ACKNOWLEDGMENTS

Many individuals generously contributed to this work over its many years of gestation, but special mention must be made of Herbert Bloom, Senior Editor, ALA Books, whose determination and patience propelled *The Librarian's Thesaurus* to completion.

Special thanks are also due Peter Hiatt, Graduate School of Library and Information Science, University of Washington, who, while director of the school, mediated the interest of the editor and publisher. He also critiqued the manuscript as it progressed through many stages and offered valued advice and support. Mae Benne, of the same university, also generously provided her knowledge and comments. Gerald W. Lundeen, School of Library and Information Studies, University of Hawaii, reviewed section C.

Artwork for the figures in section C was prepared by the University of Hawaii Design Guild.

INTRODUCTION

One major characteristic of a profession is its development and use of terminology in ways unique to practitioners of that profession. Use of a common language provides a bond among its members and reinforces a sense of belonging, of membership in a select group. Collegiality enriches the profession as a whole. An important part of the initiation of new members into a profession is the instillment of this special terminology. The language of a profession defines its scope and purpose. Once the special terms are incorporated into a new practitioner's thinking, he or she should begin to view the profession in the same way that more experienced professionals do and to achieve a common understanding and communication with others in the same field.

Librarianship, a recognized profession for over a hundred years, has developed a rich store of terminology that helps give it and its members a distinct identity. The field of librarianship, and its coordinate profession, information science, is broad, encompassing many areas of specialization. Because of this breadth, it is difficult for newcomers to librarianship to grasp all facets of the profession easily; even experienced workers may not readily understand and appreciate what others in the same profession do and how they do it. If ideas are not clarified, communication becomes difficult, and the general goals and objectives of the profession become obscured by attention to the practices in one's own narrow field of interest. People tend to associate primarily with others who share similar interests, to attend meetings with narrow focuses, and to read only about their own areas in the growing number of specialized publications that are part of the literature of the profession.

Hence, it is important that the profession's special terminology be provided with incisive explanations of what the terms mean and how they are related. The purpose of this outline and attendant discussions is to help new students see the scope of the profession and the relation among its terms, and more experienced professionals to resolve ambiguities in terms as well as to understand the totality of the field. Because of the growth of librarianship and information science, there are few renaissance librarians and information workers who are able to see the broad picture and appreciate the overall goals and objectives of the profession once they become established in a special area of interest. The emphasis in this work is on commonalities, the aspects and features of the profession with which librarians should be familiar in order to meet their common goal—the provision of information services to the publics that support them. The same basic services must be offered, though new technologies allow library professionals to provide them more efficiently and add to them as necessary.

This work attempts to identify and explain the important concepts common to librarianship. This purpose places the work somewhere between the short definitions of terms that appear in glossaries and the lengthy discussion of subjects that appear in encyclopedias. It attempts to explain terms, not just define them. The interrelationships shown among concepts indicate their significance to all specialties, types of libraries, and publics served.

Following the outlines, organized explanation is the heart of this work, which is designed to be a thesaurus of concepts divided into three divisions: general concepts, procedures or processes, and technology. General concepts covers the structure of the profession as a whole; procedures or processes covers what members of the profession do; and technology covers the methods and devices used to perform the procedures within the profession. Short discussions of the various concepts, with an emphasis on their universality and interconnectedness, are presented. The detailed index indicates where the individual terms and concepts have been placed in the outline; extensive cross-references relate terms and show how they have been categorized.

Usages are limited to North American librarianship, though many of the concepts are common to other countries because librarians in all parts of the world undoubtedly have more similarities than they have differences. The frame of reference in which this work is placed is that of the institutionally bound professional. However, professionals working independently of any institution share many of the same goals and objectives with their colleagues in libraries. The intended audience for this work is the student struggling to understand what the profession of librarianship encompasses, what its goals and objectives are, and how it strives to achieve its purpose. But it is hoped that others with greater experience in the profession will find this approach useful and thought-provoking.

There is some criticism of the profession from outside, but much more comes from practitioners themselves who appear to be frustrated by what they consider to be the profession's lack of achievement in many areas. Librarians berate each other with great enthusiasm and energy. This work cannot solve such problems, but perhaps it will lead to greater comprehension and acceptance of the multitude of enterprises included in librarianship and result in increased understanding of what library professionals are doing and how their activities are interconnected.

Douglas L. Zweizig and Ronald R. Powell

A. GENERAL CONCEPTS

A.1 Basic library concepts

A.1.1 Information

"Information" is a core term for librarianship and has multiple meanings. Some definitions focus entirely on information's role in decision-making, for example, "information is that which aids in decision-making, which reduces uncertainty" (M. C. Yovits, *Information Science: Toward the Development of a True Scientific Discipline,* Technical Report No. 69–8, Computer and Information Science Research Center, Ohio State University, 1969). Some refer to information as that which is contained in books and other media. Others relate information to the change it makes in the receiver's internal picture, for example, Gregory Bateson's definition of a bit of information as "a difference that makes a difference" (*Step to an Ecology of Mind*; Ballantine, 1972, 272) or Brenda Dervin's "that which one finds informing" ("Useful Theory For Librarianship: Communication, Not Information," *Drexel Library Quarterly,* July 1977, 16–32). Definitions can relate to sources of information ("a set of symbols with potential for meaning" [Sylvia G. Faibisoff and Donald P. Ely, "Information and Information Needs," *Information Reports and Bibliographies*, 5, no. 5 (1976): 3]) or to the receivers of information (Bateson's and Dervin's definitions are examples). Definitions can focus on information as an entity (by information, we mean that which is recorded in books and other media) or on the processes by which a person informs himself or herself. Two other terms, "data" and "knowledge," are frequently used interchangeably with "information." There are many definitions of these terms, and there is no consensus on how they differ. With terms of such richness, no single meaning can be stipulated

1

for general use. It is the writer's responsibility to clearly signal the intended meaning when using these terms.

A.1.2   **Information need**

The term "information need" refers to that need which library services or materials are intended to satisfy. It is assumed that the consumption of information results from a need for information. However, because an information need is in the minds of information users, the need cannot be directly observed but only inferred from observations of users' information consumption or from their responses to questions. Library planners have used community analysis (see A.8.1.5) to identify characteristics of community residents and to infer what library services and information might be most appropriate. Survey research that attempted to identify the topics of information need found in the general population user community did not produce useful results and has not been continued. The term is often used rhetorically to support the usefulness of library service.

A.1.3   **Intellectual freedom**

Intellectual freedom is a state of absolute ability to pursue any idea or expression to its limits. Freedom of inquiry and expression are seen to be constitutionally established in the United States in the First Amendment. The First Amendment has been interpreted by the Supreme Court to protect both the right to express and the right to hear, see, and know. Proponents of intellectual freedom see it as an absolute right; any restriction in intellectual freedom is seen as leading inevitably to further reduction and to eventual loss of any right to intellectual freedom. Librarians legitimately seek freedom from outside pressure so they may exercise their own judgment. Therefore, how or whether to provide that right in practice is a matter of continual controversy as the ideal confronts the realities of economics, desire for governmental security, the need for individual privacy, and offended sensibilities. The varying ability of individuals to pay for information is seen to affect the equity of access to information in society and therefore to affect an individual's ability to pursue ideas freely. One continuing topic of debate is the degree to which society should provide information access free of charge to the user.

In order to allow freedom of discussion in government councils and to provide national security, government requires some limits to outside scrutiny, and therefore some restriction in the intellectual freedom of its citizens. This natural opposition of the interests of a government and its citizens provides an active arena for the continual examination of the limits to intellectual freedom. In another area, with the growth of electronic surveillance ability and large data banks of personal information (social security, tax, law enforcement files), the tension between the need for individual privacy and the public's need to know has become acute. While institutions such as the press are interested in extending the public's access to information, those concerned with the rights of individual citizens seek to limit intrusion into personal lives.

In libraries, the issue of intellectual freedom is most often confronted when a librarian consciously refuses to purchase material that could be controversial, or when a client seeks to remove or restrict access to (that is, censor) materials thought to be offensive or harmful. Intellectual freedom is important to the professional authority of librarians, but the issue underlying the controversy focuses on the risks in allowing intellectual freedom versus the risks in restricting intellectual freedom. Libraries and other institutions concerned with providing information, such as schools and the press, are continually involved in this debate, both internally within the institution and externally with other institutions and individuals. The American Library Association, with its Office for Intellectual Freedom, has expressed its position in the Library Bill of Rights and in a series of interpretative statements applying the Library Bill of Rights to specific issues. Its strong positions expand the autonomy of librarians in matters of selection and access.

A.1.4 Information studies

As information is increasingly recognized as a pervasive force in modern life, the study of information questions is being conducted from a variety of disciplinary perspectives. The set of systematic approaches to the study of information phenomena and issues has been referred to by some as "information studies," and the term has been used in the names of academic programs of library education to signal a broad concern with the insights that a variety of disciplinary approaches can bring. More traditionally, the terms "library science" and "information science" have been used to delineate areas of emphasis; "information studies" is a collective term covering both.

A.1.4.1 Library science

Library science is the practice and study of the gathering, storing, retrieving, and providing of information records. Its concerns have been delimited by its identification with the library institution, and some have accused that the field lacks a conceptual base since the field's origins came from practice and not theory. In the classroom, Ralph Shaw customarily referred to library science as "a technology without a science." The variety of policies and practices that institutions employ supports his assertion. The institutional focus is reflected in the typology that follows in A.2 on type of library as a major descriptor of the field of library science.

A.1.4.2   Information science

"Information science" is the term used to describe insights into library and information phenomena and methods for information processing that have resulted from the application of a variety of scientific disciplines, such as mathematics and psychology, to information questions. Because this application has been aided by and has coincided with the dramatic growth of automation within information practice, information automation is often identified with information science, but the appropriateness of this link is a matter of contention within the field. In fact, defining the field has been a sizeable preoccupation. With Wellisch's analysis of 39 definitions of information science in 1972 ("From Information Science to Informatics: A Terminological Investigation," *Journal of Librarianship,* July 1972, 157–87), one might expect that the question would have been exhausted if not settled, but Alvin Schrader's "In Search of a Name: Information Science and Its Conceptual Antecedents" (*Library and Information Science Research, An International Journal,* July–September 1984, 227–71) gives evidence that the discussion continues. With a growing number of disciplines evidencing interest in the topic and with the increasing sophistication of the technology associated with it, it does not appear that the discussion will soon cease.

A.1.5   **Copyright**

Copyright is the right granted by a government to the authors of works so they will be guaranteed a return that will compensate them for their effort and encourage them to continue creating. At the present time, copyright law restricts the right to make copies of the copyrighted work for the life of the author plus 50 years, though there are some exceptions that are believed not to seriously injure the value of copyright. Publications of United States government agencies are, by law, not copyrighted; other governments and nongovernment publishers can and do copyright their publications.

The concept of "fair use," developed many years ago, allowed copies of works to be made if it was judged that they would not infringe upon the copyright owner's rights and that scholarship would be aided. At that time, copying already printed materials was difficult and time consuming. However, with the advent of technologies that permitted copies of existing material to be made quickly and inexpensively, such as photocopying machines (see C.1.5), copyright owners believed that the vast number of copies being made threatened their economic survival. As a consequence, the United States copyright law was revised in 1976. Fair use, though not specifically defined, was codified into section 107, which permitted copying for certain specified purposes, with specific requirements to be met. In addition, section 108 covered rights specifically granted to libraries.

A.2   **Types of libraries**

Libraries are generally categorized according to their primary clientele or the institution they are mandated to serve. There is a lack of unanimity, however, regarding specific categories. The *American Library Directory* (Bowker, 1983) employs the following nine categories of libraries: public, junior college, college and university, armed forces, government, special, law, medical, and religious. It does not include school library media centers. The *ALA World Encyclopedia of Library and Information Services* (ALA, 1980) lists eight categories: academic, archives, law, medical, national, public, school/media centers, and special.

Research libraries might represent yet another category. Research libraries are those agencies that have collections that are comprehensive enough or have enough depth to support serious scholarly investigation or research. They may be associated with an institution such as a university, may take the form of a special collection within a larger library, may be considered a special library, or may be a major urban library. The Association of Research Libraries (ARL) comprises over a hundred libraries with the common goal of strengthening research library resources and services in support of higher education and research. Membership in ARL is limited to libraries that meet a variety of size criteria. Most members are university libraries, but libraries such as the Library of Congress, the New York Public Library, and the Linda Hall Library also belong.

The typology used here is predominantly an institutional one and uses the generic term "library," ignoring the term's etymological identification with the book. This decision was made because "library" continues to be widely used, although alternate terms are adopted in some settings. For example, "media center" is used to emphasize the multimedia nature of a collection; "information agency" to focus on service rather than on materials; and "learning resource center" to highlight the role of the library in the learning process. A case could also be made for including yet another category—nonlibrary information agencies such as clearinghouses, indexing and abstracting services, information brokerages, and so on. Such agencies, however, were determined to be beyond the scope of this section.

A.2.1   **Public libraries**

Conceptually, a public library is an agency established by a municipality, county, or region to provide materials and services to all residents within the jurisdiction. In some cases, "public library" is legally defined by state statutes. Funding for public libraries comes primarily from the local jurisdiction, with state and federal sources possibly providing additional funding. The director of a public library typically reports to a library board or board of trustees appointed by the chief executive of the jurisdiction.

The basic philosophies or principles that have guided the development of public library collections and services have varied over time and from library to library. Regarding collections, top priorities have ranged from developing collections of the highest quality possible, to building well-rounded collections, to a "give 'em what they want" policy. Service priorities have ranged from concentrating on the needs of actual library users to providing outreach services in order to attract and serve those who are not library users.

The 1979 mission statement of the Public Library Association (*The Public Library Mission Statement and Its Imperatives for Service;* 1979) identifies four roles for the public library. "The public library can make a unique contribution as (1) a nontraditional educational agency mediating between the total record of human experience and the individual, (2) a cultural agency fostering creativity, enjoyment of literature and the arts, and appreciation for America's pluralistic culture, (3) an information agency providing a bridge between the individual and community resources and between the multiplicity of disciplines within the record, and keys to the wisdom in the record, and (4) a rehabilitation agency helping to bring the handicapped and deviant people in society to their full potential." The 1987 *Planning and Role Setting for Public Libraries; A Manual of Options and Procedures* gives particular emphasis to the need for a library to intentionally focus on a limited number of possible roles. Eight roles that public libraries can perform (community activities center, community information center, formal education support center, independent learning center, popular materials library, preschoolers' door to learning, reference library, and research center) are detailed in the manual with the recommendation that a public library attempt to provide services in support of no more than three or four roles.

A.2.2   Academic libraries

Academic libraries are characterized by the institutions of higher education with which they are associated. In the 1970s, the Carnegie Foundation for the Advancement of Teaching developed a scheme for classifying institutions of higher education (see *A Classification of Institutions of Higher Education,* revised edition; The Carnegie Foundation for the Advancement of Teaching, 1976.) Its classification includes categories for doctorate-granting institutions, with two subcategories of research universities; comprehensive universities and colleges; liberal arts colleges; two-year colleges and institutes; professional schools and other specialized institutions; and institutions for nontraditional study. Academic libraries are generally grouped in three broad categories: university, college, and two-year college libraries. Two-year college libraries are also referred to as community college and junior college libraries.

The mission of an academic library generally reflects the mission of its parent institution, and its collections and services are developed accordingly. For example, the library of a large research university will tend to develop a collection, the primary goal of which is to support the research activities of faculty and research staff while maintaining at least adequate resources for students. In contrast, the library of a four-year, undergraduate college will build and maintain a collection with the primary, if not only, goal of supporting the college's curriculum. Two-year community college libraries may have the most complex mission of the three. They must support the educational needs of students who plan to continue their education in a bachelor's degree program as well as those who will terminate their formal education with a two-year or associate's degree. Community college libraries must also meet the informational needs of part-time students interested in continuing or adult education only. These libraries tend to acquire a greater proportion of instructional materials, including audiovisual resources, and as a result are sometimes referred to as learning resource centers.

Generally, the academic library director reports to the college's or university's president or its chief academic officer. The director may be advised by a faculty library committee. Private academic libraries often restrict use of their materials and services to persons enrolled in or employed by their institution. Public academic libraries tend to provide at least some level of service to the general public and may even be mandated to serve as resources for the citizens of their state as well as their academic community.

A.2.3   **Archives**

Archives, as materials, are essentially those records of an organization that are considered to be worth preserving and that are best described and stored by origin or provenance. Hence, archives, as a type of library, are the agencies responsible for collecting and maintaining the records of organizations. Historically, archives were not always thought of as libraries, in large part because they tended to limit their role to a custodial one. More recently however, archives have become more service-oriented and more concerned with facilitating the use of their collections, particularly by researchers. Present-day archival services include limited reference service, photoduplication, and some lending. The growing use of automated record management techniques by both archives and libraries has blurred the distinction between the two as well.

Archives can be found at federal, state, and local governmental levels as well as within a variety of public and private organizations. They

7

are sometimes associated with a department of a library, but more likely they exist as a separate information agency. State archives are often located on the campus of the major state university and in some cases are housed within the university library, but the director of the archives is more likely to report to the state government than to the university librarian. Academic librarians seldom have formal responsibility for the archives of their own institution. Funding for archives typically comes from the institutions or governments they serve.

A.2.4   **School library media centers**

School library media centers are those agencies charged with meeting the informational needs of institutions of elementary and secondary education. They are sometimes mandated by state law. *Information Power: Guidelines for School Library Media Programs,* the 1988 document prepared by the American Association of School Librarians and the Association for Educational Communications and Technology, states that the school library media specialist should offer access to the school library media center during and beyond the school day; provide adequate resources and assistance in locating information; and guide users in selecting appropriate materials. The specialist should also provide necessary retrieval systems for the media center's contents; instruct students so they will have the necessary skills, knowledge, and attitudes concerning information access; and act as instructional consultant to teachers in curriculum development and the use of technology. The possible roles of the media specialist as a type of teacher, often in a setting of technology, are defined in some models of instructional design. All of these models divide instruction into specific functions, which are assigned to members of a teaching team.

The collections and services of the school library media center are closely associated with the instructional program of the school. Professional staff of the media center often must be certified as teachers as well as librarians (or media specialists). Materials for the center are to a large extent selected and retained on the basis of their contribution to instructional effectiveness and to meeting educational objectives. The center's staff members are able to fulfill the functions mandated by *Information Power* only if the administration and teachers recognize the contributions that staff can make to meeting the instructional objectives of the programs and consider them equal partners in the educational process. School library media centers have tended to incorporate a wide range of audiovisual and instructional media and are often referred to as instructional media centers or learning resource centers.

A.2.5   **Special libraries**

There continues to be a lack of unanimity regarding the definition of a "special library." The broadest definition includes all libraries other than public, school, and academic libraries. This definition, however, fails to consider the many special libraries, such as health science, business, and law libraries, that can be found in academic settings. More limited definitions restrict special libraries to those serving narrowly defined clientele or providing information in a limited subject area. The *Encyclopedia Americana* (1985) states that a library is "special" when (1) its collection is of a specialized nature, (2) it serves a specialized body of users, (3) it has a staff with specialized training in a particular subject matter or methodology, or (4) it offers specialized— usually personalized—services. The *ALA Glossary of Library and Information Science* (ALA, 1988) states that a special library is: "A library established, supported, and administered by a business firm, private corporation, association, government agency, or other special-interest group or agency to meet the information needs of its members or staff in pursuing the goals of the organization. Scope of collections and services is limited to the subject interests of the host or parent institution." Many special libraries are operated by businesses, industries, and research agencies. Others are essentially autonomous and serve virtually anyone needing access to their collections. Some special libraries, as noted above, are affiliated with a larger academic library system. Special libraries also serve professional organizations and societies, institutions such as prisons and hospitals, and special populations such as the blind.

Special libraries are characterized by their close adaptation of materials and services to the organization or clientele they serve. They tend to concentrate on immediate needs of their patrons and, especially in the for-profit sector, must continually justify their activities to their parent company or funders. In some cases, special libraries must devise organizational schemes to accommodate highly specialized materials such as laboratory reports, clippings, offprints, and photographs. Special libraries generally provide more intensive, personalized information services than do libraries with larger, more diverse clientele. These services often take the form of current awareness or selective dissemination of information and may include lists of new acquisitions, summaries of literature, routing of journals, customized searches, and even analysis and evaluation of literature. In short, special libraries do everything within their means to provide the information needed by their parent organization or primary clientele. Many librarians who work in academic libraries with these characteristics are considered by the Special Library Association and by themselves to be special librarians.

A.2.6   **Government libraries**

Many libraries serving governmental agencies can be considered special libraries (see A.2.5) in that they collect materials in narrowly defined areas and serve specific clienteles. But governmental agencies also support libraries with more general purposes. Examples are most often found at the federal and state levels. At the federal level, the Library of Congress serves its primary clientele, the U.S. Congress, but also provides a variety of services to the national library community. Chief among these services is the provision of bibliographic information in machine- (computer) readable form and in print. The Library of Congress is the closest thing the United States has to a national library. Other libraries at the federal level with somewhat more focused missions include the National Library of Medicine as well as libraries designed chiefly to serve a specific agency such as the State Department Library and the Defense Communication Agency Library.

At the state level, a library may well serve a variety of state agencies, including other libraries and the general public as well as the state legislature (see A.3.3). State law libraries (which may be affiliated with the state library) and state historical agencies may also serve a variety of constituencies. Individual governmental agencies may have their own libraries or office collections as well. In addition to collecting and organizing materials in their areas of interest, government agency libraries also generally have responsibility for obtaining and organizing internal agency documents.

A.3   Types of library organization

A.3.1   Networks

Two or more libraries can work together for a variety of purposes, generally involving the sharing or distribution of materials, information, or services. Such cooperative groups can include a range of formality in their organization. A general term for such organized cooperation is "library network"; other terms used are "consortium," "cooperative," and "federation." A network can be characterized by the geographic area it covers (a statewide network), by a common technology (a computer network), by a type of library focus (special library network), or by another common feature. In a more limited definition, a network is an organization of libraries formed for specific functions, such as automated circulation, sharing of bibliographic records, or interlibrary resource sharing. The governance of networks is usually limited to the specific function of the network, whereas the governance of a library system (see A.3.2) may address the full range of the library's functions.

A.3.2   Systems

A library system is a comprehensive formal organization of libraries for the purpose of cooperative and coordinated services that can take different governance structures. The two basic models for governance are the federated system and the consolidated system, although local history and conditions can modify the basic model used.

A.3.2.1   Federated

A federated library system is a collective of libraries that has its own administration and in which individual members retain their own autonomy. Members receive funding from individual sources and have individual administrations. The system's administrative function is to provide centralized services and to promote cooperation among its members. In fact, the term "cooperative system" is often used to describe systems with this structure. System services may include interlibrary delivery, continuing education programs, centralized processing, consulting services, and centralized automation. Federated systems are the form often used for multitype cooperation.

A.3.2.2   Consolidated

A consolidated library system is a collective of libraries in which the direction for the system's member libraries comes from a central system administration. Funds for the member libraries are distributed through the system administration. In addition to the services provided by federated systems, consolidated system services include centralized planning of facilities and services, personnel administration, and centralized budgeting.

A.3.3   **State library agencies**

State library agencies are administrative agencies at the state level that perform such functions as administering federal funds provided through the Library Services and Construction Act, administering state aid to libraries, providing expertise in such areas as construction and library automation, administering standards for library service (see A.8.4), providing library services to state government (see A.2.6) and to resident institutions, administering certification of librarians, developing and administering state legislation for libraries, and providing continuing education for library staffs and trustees. Historically, state library agencies have been most closely associated with public libraries. Where the state library agency is associated with the state education department, direct involvement with school media centers may also be provided through the state library agency. The current development in some states is for state library agencies to relate to all libraries in the state and to foster the creation of multitype library systems (see A.3.2.1). Such systems provide coordinated central services (such as interlibrary delivery) and administer cooperative agreements among libraries.

A.3.4   **Library associations**

A.3.4.1   Of individuals

Librarians and others interested in library matters form associations in their mutual interest. The purposes of associations can be to provide a forum for sharing professional information, to provide continuing education, to represent the interests of the association in the political arena, to promote the publication of professional tools and literature, to support the work of members, and to provide the opportunity for associating with others of like interests. Library associations can focus on type of library, geographical region, type of service offered, or type of information handled.

A.3.4.2   Of libraries or library agencies

Libraries are able to hold institutional membership in many library associations, and many do so in order to efficiently obtain association publications and other membership benefits. One association composed entirely of library members is the Association of Research Libraries, an invitational organization consisting of the largest libraries in the United States. The Chief Officers of State Library Agencies is another association with members that are institutions rather than individuals. In these cases, the associations are formed to promote the interests of these types of library institutions.

A.4   **Library constituencies**

The constituencies of a library are the individuals or groups that have an interest in or influence on the library. They may be internal to the library, that is, inside the library organization, or external to the library, outside the organization and having influence on it.

A.4.1   **Internal constituencies**

Library staff compose those constituencies inside the library organization. The American Library Association's "Library Education and Personnel Utilization Statement" (1976) provides standard terminology for staff categories and proposes a structure for the relationships among these categories.

A.4.1.1   Staff without professional library degree

Libraries employ a variety of staff to perform functions that support the mission of the library but do not require a professional degree. These functions include the processing of materials, routine compilation of bibliographic records, and security, maintenance, secretarial, accounting, personnel, and circulation procedures. These staff members are sometimes paid hourly wages and work under the direct supervision of professional staff. Staff members with professional preparation in other fields, such as personnel or public relations, may be salaried and classified with professional staff. In small libraries, there may be no staff with a professional library degree. Consulting services may be provided in these cases by library system or state library agency staff.

A.4.1.2   Staff with professional library degree

While certification for the library professional is rarely written into law (with the exception of school library media specialist certification), the American Library Association and individuals and institutions associated with librarianship strongly agree that professional status is designated by the Master in Library Science degree, usually with the qualifier that the degree be awarded by a program accredited by the American Library Association.

Staff members with the professional library degree are generally allowed greater autonomy in planning and implementing their tasks, are presumed to have some accountability to their profession as well as their employers, are given supervisory responsibility for staff without professional credentials, and are given some voice in the library's policy-making.

A.4.1.3   Administration

In large libraries, staff members may be designated as administration or management. Such staff members are charged with the overall direction of the library, with planning and goal-setting, with preparation of budget submissions, with selection and review of staff, and with reporting to the governing body. In small libraries, administrative functions are performed by individuals who also have direct service responsibilities.

A.4.2   **External constituencies**

External constituencies consist of those individuals or groups outside the library that have an actual or potential interest in the library. They may be grouped in categories such as funders, governors, users, potential users, and nonusers. Those who fund, use, and govern the library are organized into political structures that create policy for libraries. The professional latitude that libraries require must be exercised within constraints.

A.4.2.1   Governance

Governance refers to the individuals or groups to which a library is directly accountable, often those determining the library's funding (see A.8.2). In school settings, the school principal and perhaps the head of media services for the school district provide the governance. In public library settings, in most states immediate direction regarding a library's policy, budgeting, and personnel matters comes from the board of trustees. The board of trustees may be an administrative board, in which case it is legally responsible for the public library's actions. Alternatively, the board of trustees could serve as an advisory board; the library would be treated as a department of city or county government, similar to the police, fire, and parks and recreation departments. In such cases, the city or county administrator would hold legal responsibility for the library.

An academic library director or administrator will report to an administrative officer such as a provost and may also sit with the council of deans. An advisory faculty committee, which could include student participation, may also be part of the governance and represent the users.

A.4.2.2   Population served

Population served is the primary population that a library is mandated to serve. A public library's population served would be the people of the community from which the library receives its primary funds. For an academic library or a school library media center, it would be the students, faculty, and staff of the institution. The population served by a special library may be the employees of the sponsoring organization, the membership of the association served, or other designated groups.

A.4.2.3   Users

Users are those who actually use the library according to some definition of use, such as those who visit the library one or more times a year. Library managers and researchers are interested in the characteristics of those who use the services most frequently and the activities of users while in the library. Library managers are also concerned with those persons in the potential user population who have not become users of a library's services.

A.5   Library education

There are many types of educational programs preparing people to work in different types of libraries and information agencies. The American Library Association's Committee on Accreditation (COA) officially accredits only master's level programs (see A.5.2.1), but the Association also has a Standing Committee on Library Education (SCOLE), that provides representation for all types of programs. Graduate library schools offering accredited master's level programs are institutional members of the Association for Library and Information Science Education (ALISE).

A.5.1   Undergraduate library education

While undergraduate institutions may offer courses designed to help students become more effective users of libraries, the emphasis in this section is on programs that prepare students to be employed in libraries. Full programs in library education at the community college level train students to work as library technical assistants. These are

14

vocational education programs that give students a sense of library services and train them to perform routine operations in the processing of materials, circulation procedures, and other support features.

Undergraduate programs may offer a bachelor's degree in library science and are usually aimed at preparing students to serve in school library media centers. Undergraduate library education is usually not considered adequate preparation for professional positions, and few undergraduate courses receive credit in the master's curriculum. At the present time, libraries do not specify associate or bachelor degrees as requirements for employment, although some exceptions are made where there is a strong program at a local undergraduate institution. In libraries, there is no clear job progression for persons with undergraduate degrees. Persons with such preparation are generally restricted to positions designated as nonprofessional or paraprofessional.

The newer undergraduate programs in information studies are intended to prepare persons for employment in information-related positions in nonlibrary agencies or to provide preparation for graduate study in other information-related professions, such as law.

A.5.2   Graduate library education

A.5.2.1   Master's level

Professional status in librarianship is conventionally attained with the Master of Library Science. Courses in a master's degree program will include concepts basic to the field as well as practical skills in organizing and retrieving information and in the planning of programs of service. In 1990, sixty-one institutions in the United States and Canada offered master's degrees accredited by the American Library Association. (A listing of accredited library schools with indication of which offer post-master's or doctoral programs is available from ALA's accreditation officer.) Accreditation involves the periodic writing of a self-study document by the library school and a visit to the school by a team appointed by the ALA Committee on Accreditation. In addition, annual reports are sent to the committee.

The American Library Association accredits master's programs only. Undergraduate, post-master's, and doctoral programs receive no accreditation specific to the field of librarianship. In addition to the accredited programs, many master's degree programs exist that are not accredited and that do not seek accreditation. These programs often prepare librarians for a specific type of library (accreditation has implied broader preparation of librarians for more than one type of library) and expect that their graduates will be hired by local employers for whom the program has credibility. Advertised professional position descriptions usually specify an MLS from an accredited program.

15

A.5.2.2   Post-master's level

As their interests and responsibilities change, librarians with a master's degree in library science often take additional courses throughout their careers to study new areas or to bring their knowledge up to date. Some library schools offer study programs for professional librarians who can commit an additional year of study to a topic of interest. Such programs often lead to a Certificate of Advanced Study, or a Specialist Degree (that is, a sixth-year degree). Such study frequently includes non-library science subjects needed by the practitioners to meet their professional responsibilities and to improve their performance.

A.5.2.3   Doctoral level

The doctoral degree in library and information studies generally involves at least two years of coursework beyond the master's degree and is intended to prepare students for library education careers, for policy-making positions, or for research or consulting activities. Many doctoral degree programs require that the student pass a comprehensive examination. Doctoral programs with the purpose of preparing library administrators may offer a Doctor of Library Science degree. Doctoral programs with an emphasis on research will award the Doctor of Philosophy degree and will concentrate on obtaining research skills and preparing a research dissertation.

A.5.3   **Continuing library education**

Continuing education generally is not degree-oriented. It is provided through workshops, professional association meetings, or even professional publications, all of which help maintain existing skills or add new competencies and knowledge. Academic credit may or may not be given for formal courses with professional content. Continuing education may be provided by an employer directly or paid for by the employer, or the costs may be borne by the librarian. The term "staff development" is sometimes used to designate continuing library education conducted by an institution to strengthen its employees' capacities in their present positions. Such training is generally the responsibility of the institution. A few studies have been performed to determine where librarian needs for further continuing education lie. The Continuing Library Education Network and Exchange (CLENE) is a forum for the exchange of ideas and material on continuing education.

A.6   **Research concepts**

A.6.1   **Units of analysis**

"Unit of analysis" is a technical term for the item that is tallied in research. It should not be confused with the topic of research. For example, a researcher investigating how a library is used gathers information about individual users. Library use is the topic of the research; library users are the units of analysis. Units of analysis are those units that must first be described in order to aggregate their characteristics for the purpose of describing some larger group or explaining some concept or activity. Units of analysis can be individuals, groups, organizations, or things such as books and cataloging records.

A.6.2   **Variables**

A "variable" can be defined as a concept that can assume any one of a range of values. It might be more accurate, however, to view a variable as a measurable representation of a concept. For example, "library use" could be considered a concept or an abstract term referring to all types of library use. On the other hand, "circulation" could be treated as a more concrete, measurable type of library use. "Circulation" could take on any value ranging from zero circulations to the highest number of circulations per person or library.

Variables are the building blocks of hypotheses. The hypothesis provides the framework for the variables or explains what relationship, if any, exists between or among the variables being investigated. For example, one might hypothesize that increasing the number of access points for a title in a library's catalog will result in greater use of that title. In this case, one is hypothesizing a causal relationship; "access points" is the independent variable and "use" the dependent variable. Independent variables are also referred to as predictor variables or, in experimental research, as experimental variables. Dependent variables are sometimes called subject variables.

In order for variables to be measured, they must be operationally defined. Returning to the previous example, one might define "circulation" as the number of books borrowed by undergraduate students at a particular university during a specified time period. The definition of the initial concept or variable is now concrete and detailed enough to indicate how library use will actually be measured. If one wanted to measure additional aspects of library use, it would be necessary to develop additional operational or working definitions for activities such as using the library catalog, asking reference questions, and so on.

A.6.3   **Measurement**

A.6.3.1   Levels of measurement

As discussed in the preceding section, a researcher ultimately must define variables operationally so they can be measured, at least in quantitative research. There are different ways to measure variables, depending on the characteristics of the variables. These different methods may be referred to as data levels, levels of measurement, or scales of measurement. The data levels used determine the amount of information collected and the statistics that can be used to describe and analyze the information.

The most basic level of data is nominal data. Data at this level are simply indicators of the classes into which items fall. For example, data describing the colors of cars, the gender of respondents to a survey, or service desk use at a library are nominal. Numbers would be arbitrarily assigned as codes to indicate different colors, genders, or service desks. The appropriate summary statistic would indicate the class into which most cases fall. The mode, for example, would indicate the most popular car color, which gender occurred more frequently among survey respondents, or which service desk was used most.

Nominal data are organized in no particular order. However, the next level of data—ordinal data—refers to data that, in addition to discriminating between cases in terms of some characteristic, also imply an order. An example would be sizes of cars: subcompact, compact, intermediate, full-size. The code number 1 is assigned to the smallest size, subcompact; 2 to the next size; and so on. Therefore, a value of 2 for car size indicates a car larger than a car with a value of 1 and smaller than a car with a value of 3. An ordinal level of data implies order only; it does not indicate, for example, how much larger or smaller one car is than another.

Many library survey questions produce data that ranks preferences for service or data that reflects knowledge of library services. The appropriate summary statistic indicates how many cases fell above or below a particular value. For example, the median indicates how many cases fall above or below the midpoint of the considered scores. A percentile score indicates what percentage of scores fell below the percentile score.

The next level of data, interval data, not only implies an order, but also has equal intervals between successive values. For example, on the Fahrenheit scale, a degree interval has been defined so that each degree measures the same amount of temperature change. Thus, the difference between 30 degrees F and 31 degrees F is the same as the difference between 209 degrees F and 210 degrees F. The appropriate summary statistic would indicate the score produced by dividing the sum of the scores by the number of scores summed, that is, the arithmetic mean.

The highest level of data, ratio data, has the quality of interval data with the additional characteristic of having a true value of zero. Examples are data relative to weight, distance, and money. That is, it is possible to have zero weight, zero distance, and zero money. Therefore, in addition to being able to add and subtract ratio data (to say that one weight, for example, is a specific amount greater or less than another), it is also possible to multiply or divide ratio data. It makes sense to say one object weighs twice as much as another; it does not make sense to say that it is twice as hot today as it was yesterday. Ratio data are found in library studies when absolute counts, such as counts of users and items are used. A full range of arithmetic and statistical calculations are legitimate with ratio data.

A.6.3.2   Validity and reliability

As discussed in the preceding section, the measurement of phenomena represents one of the major activities of quantitative research. But it is not enough to measure a phenomenon quantitatively; it must be measured validly as well. A researcher must be satisfied that he or she has measured what was supposed to be measured. For example, if a librarian used a test to measure library skills, he or she should be concerned with whether the test measured all of the different skills of importance to the research. In addition, the librarian should be confident that the test was not actually measuring some other factor such as intelligence or attitude. In other words, the means of measurement must be valid.

It is also important that measurements be reliable. A test or an item on a questionnaire, for example, should consistently measure whatever it is supposed to measure. Generally speaking, a measure is considered reliable if its margin of error is small and does not fluctuate much from one observation to another.

Validity and reliability are also important to the design of a research study. If a research study's measures are deemed valid, this probably means that the researcher has accurately identified or labeled the variables being studied, that the researcher has correctly addressed the causal relationships being tested, and that these findings can be generalized to other comparable situations. A research study high in reliability tends to produce results that are repeatable or replicable. Reliable conclusions are more easily generalized as well.

A.6.4   **Sampling**

Sampling is a technique that allows a researcher to describe or make inferences about a large group or population by studying a relatively small subset or sample of that population. It is more economical to study a sample than it is to examine every member of the total group; in some cases, it is not even possible to examine the entire population. As librarians must often deal with large groups (catalogs of bibliographic records, shelves of books, populations of library users and nonusers, and so on), sampling can be an important, if not critical, skill.

There are essentially two types of sampling methods— nonprobability sampling and probability sampling. In selecting a nonprobability sample, the investigator cannot state the statistical probability that a specific member of the population will be included in the sample. In fact, certain members of the population may have no probability or chance of being selected for the sample. Consequently, the researcher cannot be confident that the sample accurately represents the population from which it was drawn and has to be cautious about describing the population based on what is known about the sample. For example, if a researcher were conducting an exit interview in a library and simply interviewed the first hundred people that he or she could stop, then the resulting sample would be a nonprobability sample. On the other hand, if the researcher systematically interviewed persons leaving the library in such a way that every library user over a specified period of time had an equal chance of being interviewed, then the sample would be a probability sample. Assuming that the sample were large enough, the researcher could be more confident about describing the population of library users based on what was learned about the sample users and could employ a greater range of statistics in doing so.

A.6.5   **Data analysis**

A.6.5.1   Descriptive and inferential statistics

Before analyzing data collected during an investigation, a researcher should decide the purpose(s) of the analysis. If a researcher desires to do no more than summarize and describe the data, then descriptive statistics would be in order. More specifically, descriptive statistics can be used to present the characteristics of the data vis-à-vis graphs, charts, and tables; indicate the central tendency of the data; indicate how widely the data are dispersed; measure the relationship between or among different variables in the data; and describe differences between or among groups.

Common measures of central tendency are the mean (average score), the median (middle score), and the mode (most frequently occurring score). Conventional examples of measures of dispersion are the range of scores, the mean and standard deviations of scores, and the variance of scores.

In contrast to descriptive statistics, inferential or inductive statistics can be used to predict or estimate characteristics of a population based on known characteristics of a sample of the population and to test hypotheses using tests of statistical significance. Certain inferential statistics are classed as parametric statistics, which require that the data to be analyzed are distributed normally (that is, when plotted on a graph, they produce a normal curve). Other inferential statistics, referred to as nonparametric statistics, are considered to be distribution-free and do not require the assumption of a normal population. However, parametric statistics are considered to be more powerful and generally are preferred when appropriate.

In either case, specific statistics should not be employed unless the necessary conditions are met. For example, some statistical tests require interval-level data; some are intended for analyzing two variables, others for more than two variables; and some statistics require that a distinction be made between the independent and dependent variables.

A.7   Research approaches

A.7.1   Basic research

"Basic research" is a term often used interchangeably with "pure," "theoretical," or "scientific" research. Typically, the major intent of someone conducting basic research is to create knowledge. It is generally accepted that if a profession is to continue to advance, it must be grounded on a solid body of knowledge, such as is produced by rigorous, ongoing basic research. Basic research is characterized by an adherence to an objective, systematic, often quantitative approach traditionally referred to as the scientific method of inquiry. The steps usually composing the scientific research method are: identify the research problem or topic; identify or construct a relevant theory; develop a hypothesis or tentative solution to the problem; gather the necessary information or data; analyze the data; and interpret the results.

Most of the steps or elements of the scientific method are either self-explanatory or are treated elsewhere in this text. Theory and hypothesis may warrant further discussion at this point, however. A theory is a set of statements that identify the facts, assumptions, and variables relevant to a research problem. Ideally, the theory identifies possible relationships among the key variables and suggests how and why they are related. The hypothesis, simply stated, is a tentative or proposed solution to a problem. The hypothesis helps guide or focus a research study by identifying the specific relationships to be tested. Ideally, the hypothesis should be derived from the appropriate theory. Generally speaking, basic research studies should generate findings that can be generalized to comparable situations, are replicable, can be conducted in a controlled manner, and deal with phenomena that can be observed or measured.

A.7.2   Applied research

In somewhat of a contrast to basic research, applied research tends to be more pragmatic and emphasizes producing information that is immediately applicable to an actual problem in the workplace. That is not to say, however, that the results of basic research cannot have practical applications at some point nor that applied research cannot benefit basic research efforts. Their immediate priorities are what tend to set them apart, though it could be argued that basic research, by definition, is generally more rigorous.

21

Applied research, particularly when used as a management tool, is often referred to as action research. The basic steps of action research have been identified as: identify the problem; review the relevant literature; formulate a hypothesis; design the study or setting; collect appropriate data; and evaluate the results. As can be seen, these steps are quite similar to those often followed in basic research studies. In applied research, if some aspect of an organization is being investigated, then members of that organization are often involved in the design and implementation of the study.

A.7.3   Operations research and systems analysis

Operations research (OR) is a specific type of applied research and in many cases is employed as a management tool. OR began as the application of scientific method to the solution of management problems. T.E. Caywood, in 1971, defined operations research as "an experimental and applied science devoted to observing, understanding, and predicting the behavior of purposeful man–machine systems; and operations-research workers are actively engaged in applying this knowledge to practical problems in business, government, and society" (*Operations Research,* Sept. 1971, 1138). OR tends to represent a quantitative approach to the analysis of management problems.

The standard approach to using operations research involves these steps: identify the problem; develop a mathematical model of the actual phenomenon being investigated; derive an optimal solution to the problem vis-à-vis the model; design a methodology to test the model and respective solution; and gather and analyze data accordingly. The mathematical model represents a significant addition to the scientific method described earlier (see A.7.1) and is critical to the OR methodology. Its function is to simulate, often through the use of computers, the behavior of an actual system and should help visualize a complex phenomenon.

"Systems analysis" is often used interchangeably with "operations research," but it might be defined more accurately as a method that often utilizes OR techniques. Systems analysis emphasizes the importance of considering all aspects of a system and how they interact before making important management decisions. It is often conducted before implementing and in conjunction with operating an automated system.

A.7.4   Evaluation research

Evaluation, or evaluative, research represents a common type of applied research. It tends to be practical or utilitarian in nature and is generally conducted in the workplace for the purpose of assessing resources and services (see A.8.1.4). Regarding services or programs, the evaluation may take place throughout the program, at the end, or both. Ongoing evaluation research conducted during a program will focus on the process and examine how well the program is working. Evaluation conducted upon completion of a program is more concerned with the program's outcome or effects, often in relation to previously stated desired outcomes, tends to be more quantitative in nature, and may help determine whether the program will be continued.

Evaluation research often approximates the scientific method of inquiry and frequently employs the same designs and techniques as do basic research studies. The hypothesis is often implicit and assumes that the dependent variable is a desired goal.

An evaluation activity receiving a lot of attention since the early 1970s is performance measurement (see A.8.5). Performance measures indicate what was accomplished as the result of some program and thus represent a type of outcome evaluation. They focus on indicators of library output (and are often referred to as output measures) and effectiveness rather than on more traditional measures of library input such as number of volumes, staff, and so on. Performance measures are closely related to a library's impact on its community and are often concerned with user satisfaction. Examples of performance measures are circulation statistics, availability of materials, facilities usage, reference fill rate, title fill rate, and document delivery. Techniques used for measuring performance have included the collection of statistics, questionnaires, interviews, observation, unobtrusive reference questions, diaries, consumer panels, and document delivery tests.

A.7.5   Survey research

A survey is typically conducted in order to determine the present status of a given phenomenon. In other words, a survey usually gathers contemporary data, often descriptive in nature. The survey researcher has little or no control of the research setting; that is, he or she gathers information about cases, people, and so on in their natural setting and, as a result, does not have the ability to test causal relationships. On the other hand, survey research is well suited for collecting data on a large number of cases, describing those cases, investigating personal factors, and exploring possible relationships.

There are several types of surveys, ranging from sociometric to critical incident studies, but they can generally be lumped into two large categories—analytical surveys and descriptive surveys. Analytical surveys analyze phenomena in terms of their basic components. Descriptive surveys describe the current status but can also be used to estimate characteristics of a group larger than the one surveyed, make specific predictions, and explore relationships.

A variety of techniques can be used to collect survey data. The ones most commonly employed are mailed questionnaires, telephone and personal interviews, and direct observation. Each of these techniques has various strengths and weaknesses, but two of the most important criteria for evaluating data collection technique are likely response rate and accuracy of response.

Because it is not always possible, affordable, or even desirable to survey all members of a group or population, many surveys are limited to subgroups or samples. As the researcher will wish to describe the total population based on the characteristics of the sample, it is crucial that the sample be representative of the population. Generally speaking, the larger the sample the better, but formulas can be used to calculate optimum sample size and to avoid unnecessary effort and expense.

A.7.6   **Historical research**

In contrast to survey research, historical research is concerned with events that occurred in the past. Beyond mere chronology, true historical research deals with the analysis and interpretation of past events. Its main purpose is to facilitate planning by identifying basic principles that can be applied to recurring situations.

There are different types of historical research, ranging from biographical research to the history of ideas, but most historical research, especially in library and information science, is based on the study of documents. Virtually all historical documents are either primary or secondary sources. Primary sources are those documents containing reports of firsthand observations of an event or expressions of ideas. Primary sources are crucial to historical research because they increase its reliability and provide the only sound basis for conclusions. Secondary documents, on the other hand, cannot by themselves adequately support true historical research. Secondary sources are those in which an intermediary has come between the original witness and the present researcher and include reference books, reports by relatives of actual participants or observers, and so on. In selecting primary sources of information, the researcher should ascertain that they are indeed authentic and should evaluate the quantity and quality of their contents (external and internal criticism).

There is a lack of unanimity regarding how historical research should be conducted, but most historians agree that research should approximate the traditional scientific method of inquiry. There is even less agreement as to whether historical research methods can be used to investigate or test causal relationships. Obviously, the researcher must deal with events that took place in the past and has no control over how they occurred. Also, the historian must deal with multiple causation, if he or she is going to deal with causation at all. At the very least, causality is particularly difficult to establish in historical research. Another problem specifically relevant to historical research is bias. Within the context of historical research, bias could result from a failure to consider the full evidence, or data interpretation overly influenced by preconceived notions.

A.7.7   **Bibliometrics**

The term "bibliometrics" was coined by Alan Pritchard in 1969, though the concept had been discussed at least since the early 1920s. Pritchard defined bibliometrics as "the application of mathematics and statistical methods to books and other media of communication" ("Statistical Bibliography or Bibliometrics?" *Journal of Documentation,* December 1969, 349). In actual practice, the term has been used to refer both to the quantitative analysis of literature and to literature networks and management. Bibliometrics is sometimes viewed as a special type of documentary research. Some of the earliest bibliometrics studies were little more than counts of books and journals in libraries. More recent bibliometric research has lead to important principles such as Bradford's Law of Literature Scatter, Zipf's Law, Lotka's Law, and Trueswell's 80/20 Rule. Bradford's Law maintains that a small percentage of the journals in a scientific field account for a large percentage of the significant articles in that same field. Zipf's Law relates to the frequency of occurrence of words, syllables, and letters with respect to their rank, and is considered by its propounder to be a variation of the law of least effort. Lotka's Law of scientific productivity assumes that the number of papers published by scientists are measures of their contribution to science. Trueswell's 80/20 Rule suggests that a large percentage of a library collection's use is accounted for by a small percentage of the total collection.

Bibliometric techniques often employ citation analysis and have been used in a variety of collection evaluation and use studies. More specifically, bibliometric techniques have been used to rank publications in terms of importance, identify core literature, trace the diffusion of ideas, measure the impact of publications, study subject interrelationships, investigate the structure of knowledge and how it is communicated, and improve bibliographic control.

A.7.8   **Experimental research**

The primary reason for conducting experimental research usually is to test a causal relationship between or among variables. A causal relationship exists when one or more phenomena, variables, or events cause or at least influence another event. For example, a person could reasonably argue that library use will cause or at least contribute to better reading skills. In order to investigate a causal relationship, the researcher needs to exert considerable control over the research setting. Experimental research methods are best able to provide such control.

Another important feature of experimental research is the investigator's ability to manipulate or change the independent variable in order to determine the impact that such a change will have on the dependent variable. For example, a librarian might measure the library skills (the dependent variable) of a group of undergraduate students, provide them with bibliographic instruction (the independent or experimental variable), and then measure the change in library skills. Typically, in such a study, the researcher would establish an equivalent group of students (the control group) that would not be given any bibliographic instruction. A comparison of library skills of the two groups at the end of the experiment would help identify the impact of the bibliographic instruction as the independent variable.

In some ways, experimental research methods are the most rigorous available; yet experimental studies are relatively uncommon in library and information science. A reluctance to conduct experiments may be due in part to the concern that they represent somewhat artificial tests of phenomena (quasi- and preexperiments can alleviate this concern, however). Perhaps more importantly, it is relatively difficult to establish the desired control and to manipulate variables as is called for in true experimental research within an actual work setting.

A.8   Management concepts

The attempt to distinguish "management" and "administration" frequently clouds discussions of the topic. Peter Drucker, in *Management Tasks, Responsibilities, Practices* (Harper & Row, 1974), phrased a distinction that has gained wide acceptance: "Management is that activity which, at its highest level, decides on the direction an organization should take. It answers the question, 'What is the purpose of this organization?' Having asked the important questions and arrived at answers, management seeks the optimal methods that should be employed from among the available alternatives. Administration begins where management stops. It seeks to ensure that management decisions are carried out efficiently; it strives for efficiencies. Management must also decide what not to do [p. 45]." Management will decline making a change that it believes is not advantageous to the organization.

A.8.1   Planning

A.8.1.1   Mission

The mission of any type of library is its overall or basic purpose, its primary reason for existence. The mission statement is generally written in abstract terms and communicates the library's purpose to its internal and external constituencies. A mission statement should explain what the library does; differentiate it from other organizations; encourage commitment and enthusiasm; be appropriate for the situation; be reasonably ambitious; and provide guidance for related subsequent planning activities such as the development of goals, objectives, and strategies. Achieving consensus among those affected by a mission statement is an important feature. This process provides for the participation of everyone affected and is frequently the most valuable aspect of the final statement. As noted in *Planning and Role Setting for Public Libraries* (ALA, 1987), the mission statement is well suited to communicating the library's role or its profile of library services.

A Planning Process for Public Libraries (ALA, 1980) advises that the mission statement be specific to a particular library setting for a specific time period. That is, as the library and setting change, the mission statement should be revised to reflect that change. Generalized mission statements are less useful guides for subsequent planning decisions. What follows is a sample mission statement:

> The primary responsibility of the Arizona State University Libraries is the support of the current and anticipated instructional, research, and service programs of the University. Fulfilling this responsibility entails procuring, organizing, managing, and making available library resources, as well as providing access to information resources not acquired for the University Libraries' collections. [Donald Riggs, "Strategic Planning," Paper presented at a workshop sponsored by the Missouri Chapter of ACRL, Columbia, April 17, 1987, p. 2.]

A.8.1.2   Goals and objectives

Goals and objectives are essentially statements of the intended ends of library services. A goal represents an organization's general aim or direction and should be developed in response to the organization's mission. A goal statement is usually written in qualitative and abstract terms, rather than in quantitative and specific terms. Goals are typically long-term in nature and may not be bound to any time limit. In fact, they may not be realized at all. The substance of a goal is more important than the means of achieving it. For example, a goal might be "to increase the use of our collection," with no mention of ways to do so.

Goals should be convertible into manageable, measurable objectives. Unlike goals, objectives are specific. They represent the expected outcomes of certain actions and should be phrased precisely enough to allow a determination of whether the outcome was actually achieved. Objectives are often stated in terms of what is to be done, for or by whom, in what length of time, and to what standard of performance. For example, an objective might be that "a student, by the end of the fall semester, will be able to make effective use of the library's resources in preparing for his or her courses." Objectives should be attainable and thus should reflect a realistic assessment of the resources available to support their achievement. They should be short-term and should reflect and be consistent with relevant goals.

Goals and objectives, working together, provide a framework for guiding and evaluating the activities of an organization. They facilitate allocating resources and planning for the future.

A.8.1.3   Strategies

Strategies are the means or activities by which objectives are accomplished. They are what the organization, source, or program actually does. Strategies should describe, in adequate detail, the means by which particular objectives will be met. The "Strategic Plan" (March 1986 draft) of the Association for College and Research Libraries (ACRL), sets forth the following strategy: "Develop and administer national ACRL needs assessment and evaluation survey every five years and disseminate results to appropriate units." This strategy was intended to accomplish the following objective: "Create an ongoing process for assessing educational needs and evaluating the success of ACRL professional development activities." According to Donald Riggs, author of *Strategic Planning for Library Managers* (Oryx Press, 1984), the effectiveness of strategies can usually be evaluated by the following six criteria: (1) internal consistency, (2) consistency with the external environment, (3) appropriateness in view of resources, (4) acceptable degree of risk, (5) appropriate timetable, and (6) workability. Alternative strategies may be considered for the achievement of a given objective. For example, circulation per capita may be increased by a strategy of selecting more popular materials, by changing the way in which materials are shelved, by extending the library's hours, and by a number of other strategies. Riggs points out that the development of contingencies can ease the shift from one alternative strategy to another when unforeseen occurrences make such action necessary.

A.8.1.4   Evaluation

Evaluation is the process of collecting data that will assess resources, services, and performance so that improvement can occur. Evaluation is necessary if libraries are going to determine the degree to which they have achieved their goals and objectives. In fact, an organization's evaluation procedures and criteria are best developed at the same time as its goals and objectives. With the increasing demand for accountability and the need to allocate limited resources effectively, libraries are becoming more and more involved in evaluating their resources and services.

The evaluation process can take the form of formative evaluation and summative evaluation. Formative evaluation essentially involves collecting data on the extent to which a strategy is being carried out. Summative evaluation focuses on the degree to which an objective is achieved. In either case, the results of the evaluation should be fed back into the planning process.

The major objective of evaluation, particularly in recent years, often is the determination of the effectiveness of the library. Effectiveness is usually considered to be closely tied to the achievement of goals and objectives. Basic approaches to evaluating library effectiveness have often emphasized library input (number of staff, collection size, budget), library output or performance (see A.7.4 and A.8.5), and organizational dynamics (relationships between the library staff and the formal library organization). Evaluation techniques are many and varied, ranging from mathematical determinations of the effectiveness of information retrieval systems to surveys of user satisfaction.

A.8.1.5   Community analysis

Libraries exist to serve some well-defined community, which may be the citizens of a town, the faculty and students of a school or college, or the researchers of a company. Community analysis is a process of studying the group to be served (including both library users and potential users) and its environment in order to develop appropriate collections of materials and patterns of service. The process of collecting data for a community analysis can focus on individuals (that is, aggregate characteristics of members of the community), groups, businesses and agencies, and lifestyles (transportation patterns, recreational activities, economics, and so on). Specific techniques may include observing environmental characteristics, studying demographic characteristics of the community, observing present patterns of library use, analyzing the registration file of library users, analyzing relevant documents such as census reports, and interviewing key people within the community. Traditionally, community analysis has not relied heavily on more obtrusive methods of study such as surveys. The data gathered in a community analysis should be analyzed and interpreted to determine how library services may be made most responsive to community information needs. Community analysis is most useful when it results in a written report describing the outcomes of the study and a plan explaining how the library can respond.

A.8.2   **Financial management**

A second basic and critical component of library management, along with planning (see A.8.1) and personnel management (see A.8.3), is financial or fiscal management. Financial management is the process or operational activity responsible for obtaining and keeping records of the funds necessary for efficient library operation.

The sources of funding for libraries vary according to the type of library, but most libraries are taking advantage of a growing number of revenue sources. Academic libraries, for example, continue to receive most of their financial support from their parent institution but also receive income from endowments, alumni and other donors, foundations, and federal and state governmental agencies. The bulk of funding for public libraries comes from their local governments and typically is generated by property taxes, but public libraries are also looking to a growing variety of monetary sources. Federal aid, usually channeled through state library agencies, has been a particularly important source of revenue for public libraries. Another, though somewhat controversial, source of funding for many libraries comes from the fees charged for user services.

Budgeting is the principal means by which a library manager can formalize and express a plan in terms of cost. Budgets themselves can provide financial criteria for evaluating the results of planned activities and can serve as tools for coordinating a library's various activities. The budgetary process typically involves determining the level of funding, selecting the type of budget (line-item, lump sum, program) to be employed, preparing the budget, negotiating the budget with the funding agency, and administering the budget. Budgeting is usually done on a yearly cycle.

A.8.3   **Personnel management**

An essential aspect of library administration is personnel management. An older term sometimes used for this activity is "staffing," but "personnel management" better reflects the many components of this function. Personnel management typically encompasses, at the very least, recruitment and classification of employees; salary administration; training and staff development; performance evaluation; personnel policies, including grievance procedures; and possibly unionization.

Recruiting personnel should be based on current, well-developed job descriptions and normally involves formal search procedures, including advertisement of vacant positions. The selection process usually includes the use of application forms, and in some cases pre-employment tests, interviews (often with a search committee), and the verification and evaluation of an applicant's credentials. Salary administration involves determining specific salaries, developing salary scales, awarding salary increases, and weighing fringe benefits. Personnel training refers to the orientation of new employees. Training provided to employees needing new skills because of reassignments or evolving duties is usually referred to as staff development. Training that employees initiate themselves, often for purposes of career advancement, is often categorized as continuing education. Performance evaluation, not to be confused with performance or output measurement (see A.8.5), is essentially the assessment of the quantity and quality of employees' work. Personnel policies and procedures cover everything from performance evaluations, to promotions and raises, to grievances. Ideally, policies should be in writing, up to date, and distributed to all employees. Unionization occurs when the employees of an organization join or organize a labor union for the purpose of collective bargaining. Collective bargaining occurs when the employer and representatives of the employees meet at reasonable times and confer in good faith regarding wages, hours, promotion, sick leave, and other terms of employment.

A.8.4   **Standards for library service**

A standard can be defined as a gauge or criterion used to assess, for example, a library's attainment of certain levels of service, materials, facilities, and so on. Many standards deal only with minimal acceptable levels, but other levels have been considered ideals or models. Standards often have been stated in terms of input or ingredients, such as the number of books or staff members needed to provide quality service. More recently, standards have been developed that attempt to state the quality of the desired outcome of the service, such as the time within which materials should be made available by a library.

Standards are generally developed for a type of library and published and promulgated by the relevant library association (for example, "Standards for College Libraries," published by the Association of College and Research Libraries, 1986). In addition to serving as statements of acceptable or ideal levels of performance, standards have been used as measures for evaluation, as stimuli for the development and improvement of library services and collections, and as instruments to facilitate decision-making and management (see A.7.4 and A.8.1.4). Standards, as evaluative tools, have their limitations. For example, they may be perceived as ideals when in fact they were intended only as minimal acceptable levels. They may be difficult to interpret or apply due to their subjectivity or lack of precision. If an organization is going to use standards, they must be clearly stated, up to date, measurable (assuming they are quantitative-type standards), authoritative, and appropriate to the organization's goals and objectives.

Guidelines, in contrast to standards, tend to be more concerned with procedures and less likely to be used for evaluation and comparison purposes. For example, the "Guidelines for Two-Year College Learning Resources Programs" (ACRL, 1982) were "designed to provide criteria for information, self-study, and planning, not to establish minimal (or accreditation) standards...they represent recommended practices...." Guidelines have been developed for activities ranging from bibliographic instruction to screening and appointing academic librarians. Regarding the American Library Association, new standards must be approved by an ALA-level committee, while guidelines may be issued by a division of ALA.

A.8.5   **Performance or output measurement**

Traditionally, libraries have been evaluated in terms of input or available resources, such as number of volumes, number of staff members, size of facilities, and so on. More recently, there has been a vigorous movement toward evaluating libraries according to their output or performance. This latter evaluation focuses on what was accomplished with the library's resources. Many of the performance measures developed thus far have concentrated on such factors as library effectiveness, the library's impact on the community, and user satisfaction.

A considerable number of specific performance measures, many quantitative in nature, have been developed in recent years. *Output Measures for Public Libraries* (2nd ed., ALA, 1987) incorporates the following measures: circulation per capita, in-library materials use per capita, library visits per capita, program attendance per capita, reference transactions per capita, reference completion rate, title fill rate, subject and author fill rate, browsers' fill rate, registration as a percentage of the population, turnover rate, and document delivery. The performance measures identified in *A Planning Process for Public Libraries* (ALA, 1980) include overall citizen satisfaction, perceptions of non-users, and user satisfaction. The Association of Research Libraries' *Objective Performance Measures for Academic and Research Libraries* (1984) focuses on library materials availability, library materials accessibility, patron activity analysis, and specific activities delay analysis. The Association of College and Research Libraries is developing a performance measures manual comparable to *Output Measures for Public Libraries.*

As noted earlier in this section, such performance measures are better indicators of a library's effectiveness than are the more traditional measures of input only. More specifically, performance measures can provide the kind of data that helps administrators make more efficient use of limited time and materials; they can facilitate planning; they can provide some of the data needed for cost-benefit analysis; they can identify needs that are not being met; they can measure progress toward the achievement of goals and objectives; and they can, in general, help libraries be more accountable to their funding sources and constituencies. (See A.7.4 for additional discussion of performance measures.)

Mary Ellen Soper

B. Procedures or Processes

Procedures or processes performed in libraries and information centers are discussed in section B.3, but before these can be addressed, it is necessary to first describe the bibliographic universe and its parts, then the features of bibliographies, including the records that constitute such bibliographies. Library processes are all founded upon and derived from the characteristics of the bibliographic universe and the materials within it. Bibliographies, with their records, are the vital surrogates for bibliographic materials and provide control of and access to the universe.

B.1 Bibliographic universe

The bibliographic universe consists of all physical objects that record information and can be treated as entities. As such, they form the basis for bibliographic descriptions. Information can be defined broadly and in many ways (see A.1.1). If an information-bearing object cannot be recorded, it cannot be reproduced, so the bibliographic universe is limited to those objects that can be reproduced. This universe has various fundamental characteristics, each of which stands independently.

B.1.1 Bibliographic units

There are various ways of dividing the bibliographic universe into discrete units. One way, based on the work of Seymour Lubetzky, divides all information-carrying units into works and books (*Principles of Cataloging, Final Report, Phase I: Descriptive Cataloging*, Institute of Library Research, UCLA, 1969). Works consist of the intellectual content of units, and thus have no physical existence until embodied in an actual physical book. It is unfortunate that Lubetzky used the term "book" to represent the material record of a work; "book" has another much more common meaning, but as used by Lubetzky, the term encompasses all physical formats (see B.1.5) able to contain the information that makes up a work. The existence and extent of a work is defined by a creator or author; the book or books that contain a work are usually defined by the producer or publisher. Most works compose only one book, though some have long lives and a great variety of physical forms. The arrangement of the bibliographic universe into works and their physical manifestations, books, forms a basic approach to organization in the *Anglo-American Cataloguing Rules* (AACR 1st ed., ALA, 1967; 2nd ed., 1978; revision, 1989).

AACR provides rules for creating descriptions of bibliographic units (see B.2.5.1). The units discussed in AACR are the physical manifestations (in other words, the books) of works, but the concept of works is also encompassed by the rules. The various manifestations (books) of a work can be linked to the work through notes on the bibliographic record, by using uniform titles (see B.2.5.2.2.1.2), or by standardizing the headings attached to records (see B.2.5.1). Unfortunately, a bibliographic arrangement based on works and books causes problems when change in an existing work creates a new work; that is, how much variation can there be between various books of a work before these books no longer reflect the original work, but instead represent a new work?

Another way to divide the bibliographic universe into units is proposed by Patrick Wilson in *Two Kinds of Power* (University of California, 1978 reprint). He divides this universe into works, texts, and exemplars. The work (intellectual content) can consist of a group of texts, which are the ordering of certain words in a certain sequence. (Wilson limits his bibliographic universe to writings and recorded sayings, unlike Lubetzky.) The text, as a sequence of words and auxiliary symbols, is an abstract entity; it has no weight and occupies no space. There may be dozens of slightly different texts, such as numerous editions and translations, all claiming to consist of what the author created in the original work. The exemplar is the physical manifestation or form of a text. The parallel between Lubetzky and Wilson's divisions is clear, with the useful addition of Wilson's "text" to take care of variant editions and translations. In AACR, based on Lubetzky's model, a revised or updated edition is considered a new work, but translations are regarded as books of the original work.

Wilson can discover no satisfactory general rule that will sharply distinguish texts that are texts of a given work from those that are not texts of a given work. The existence of a new work still depends on the author's determination. Wilson's "exemplar" and Lubetzky's "book" are the physical units that carry information, and hence are the elements libraries deal with regularly, though the content of these units is of greater importance.

Another less important way to classify the units that make up the bibliographic universe is as bibliographic and physical units or volumes. A bibliographic volume is a unit that contains the physical manifestation of a work. A physical volume is a discrete unit that can be separated from all other units. A bibliographic volume may be contained entirely in one physical volume; it may require more than one physical volume; or it may exist together with other bibliographic volumes in one physical volume. The distinction between bibliographic and physical volumes aids libraries when they determine the size of collections of bibliographic materials, and aids users needing precision in citations. In descriptive cataloging, the distinction between bibliographic and physical volumes, if a distinction is present, appears only in the physical description area (see B.2.5.1).

B.1.2   **Patterns of publication**

Patterns of publication or production refers to whether bibliographic items are complete in one, several, or a presumed infinite number of parts. The specific pattern of publication affects how an item will be selected, purchased, organized, stored, accessed, and preserved in bibliographic facilities. Bibliographic materials fall fairly clearly into one of three general patterns of publication.

B.1.2.1   Monographic

A bibliographic item in any format that is complete in one or more physical pieces or intended to be completed in a finite number of pieces is monographically published. The producer's intention at the beginning of an item's production is the important factor; if the item has a predetermined completion point, it is a monographic item and the content is of finite length. If, however, the producer does not foresee a specific point of completion, the bibliographic item is being serially published. All bibliographic items, regardless of format, are published either monographically or serially. Monographic items are generally easier to record, control, use, and preserve because they are either complete as published or their completion date can be predicted. They are therefore less susceptible to bibliographic change.

B.1.2.2   Serial

Serially published bibliographic items are items in any format, usually published in successive physical pieces, and intended by the producer to continue indefinitely. The producer's intention is of primary importance. A serially published item may consist of only one issue before it ceases publication, but if the producer originally intended the issues to continue indefinitely, the item is still an example of the serial pattern.

Many terms have been used to describe various kinds of serials, such as "periodicals," "magazines," "newspapers," "annuals," "journals," "bulletins," "memoirs," "proceedings," "transactions," "papers," and so on. But a closer look at these terms' overlapping definitions supports the contention that there are really few useful distinctions among these serial types. "Set" and "continuation" are two more terms lacking precise and unequivocal definitions.

The pattern of succession of serial parts can be divided into periodic and nonperiodic. Periodic publication occurs when serial issues are produced at regular, predictable intervals predetermined by the producer. This predictability allows most such publications to be billed by intervals in advance of publication. Intervals between publication can range from one day on up, though the AACR definition of periodicals limits periodic serials to those issued at least once a year. Nonperiodic serials are those issued at unpredictable intervals; usually a new issue appears when the producer has enough material to produce it. Such serials are commonly paid for as new parts are produced.

Libraries generally do not provide access to the individual parts of serials; such access is usually provided by commercial indexing and abstracting services.

B.1.2.2.1   Monographic series

Monographic series, or simply series, are hybrids; while published serially, but usually not periodically, they consist of individual bibliographic units that are monographic in nature. Units in a monographic series have their own authors, titles, and dates of publication. Occasionally they may also have different publishers and formats. But these monographic publications share a series title, which gives them a common identity. Frequently parts of a monographic series share a publisher, format, and general broad subject.

Many monographic series consist of individually numbered units, though some series have no internal numbering. *Anglo-American Cataloguing Rules* does not consider unnumbered monographic series to be serials, but this distinction seems to be based primarily on the difficulty of recording such series rather than on any principle.

Because series items share a title that binds them together, they can be acquired, organized, accessed, and shelved as serials, though usually they are also given access points that bring out the uniqueness of each item in the series, and tie each item together in the same series.

B.1.3   **Publishers or producers**

Publishers or producers are responsible for making available the content of works in particular manifestations. They don't usually create the content, nor do they always assume responsibility for it. They also do not usually print the finished item, though they do edit and distribute it. The name of a publisher or producer on a publication is a sign of quality and can indicate a publication's worth.

B.1.3.1   Government

Any part of any level of any government appears to be capable of producing publications. Government publications encompass not only those originating from or published by a government agency, but also those publications that result from government expense or that are issued under a government agency's authority. Governmental publishing is a broad area with hazy boundaries between government and nongovernment publications. Government-sponsored research is often published by nongovernment bodies. Government publications are often not copyrighted and can be republished with few or no changes by nongovernment publishers. Technically, these are government produced, but in practice they may be treated as if they are not. Some agencies are clearly governmental in nature (for example, government-supported colleges and universities), but their publications are treated in libraries as if they are nongovernmental.

Defining government publications also requires a definition of government. Municipal, state, and federal levels are usually clearly definable, but other governmental organizations, such as multistate, regional, and international bodies, are not as clear-cut. Government agencies in the United States are usually required by law to communicate their decisions and actions to those they govern, and their publications are one way of meeting this requirement. The government as a producer of bibliographic items is important due to the inherent authority in such items; because many libraries use government source as a basis for organization (see B.3.4.2), the question of whether a publisher is a government agency takes on added importance.

Many governments have set up their own agencies for printing and distributing the publications of their various units. At the federal level in the United States, the Government Printing Office (GPO) prints and distributes many government agency publications; similar bodies exist in many states and in other countries. But some government agencies contract with nongovernment bodies to print and distribute their works. Such works will be copyrighted by the nongovernment publisher (see A.1.5). Publications printed and distributed by the GPO are not copyrighted.

The debate continues over whether publications derived from government-supported work should be accessible to the public at a minimal charge with no copyright restrictions or whether the government should attempt to recover some of the cost of these works by contracting with nongovernment agencies for publication, which would result in higher charges, imposition of copyright, and limited access for the public. Libraries have tended to support low or no charges with no copyright because they advocate their users' rights and needs. A segment of the public, however, prefers to reduce government costs by pricing these publications closer to what they actually cost to produce, with little or no government subsidy. This segment of the public also supports the right of nongovernmental publishers to make profits when possible, in spite of the fact that the information was produced at the taxpayers' expense.

B.1.3.2   Nongovernment

Nongovernment publishers or producers can be divided into two broad groups: commercial and noncommercial. Commercial publishers, divided into two categories, trade and mass market, are organizations that must make a profit from their activities to survive. Their major activity is the publication and distribution of bibliographic units which primarily are intended for sale through mass market outlets, bookstores, book clubs, and libraries.

Nontrade (or noncommercial) publishers are those organizations that do not concentrate primarily on publishing, but instead on some other activity. Publishing may provide a major source of support for such organizations, but publishing is not the most important objective. Rather, it serves the goals of the parent organization. These publishers often are not-for-profit organizations, such as professional and trade organizations, societies of individuals with mutual interests, and academic institutions. They are guided by service and not exclusively profit. Usually their challenge is to make small press runs financially feasible.

The distinction between commercial and noncommercial publishers can blur, due to changing circumstances. For example, many university presses, once considered noncommercial, are now enjoined by their parent institutions to be self-sufficient. They are forced to make enough profit to support themselves and can no longer rely on subsidies from their parents for survival.

B.1.4   Authorship

Traditionally, in the Anglo-American practices used to describe items in the bibliographic universe, creators or authors of bibliographic units could be either people or corporate bodies. A corporate body, defined broadly as a group of people working together for some purpose and identified by a proper name, was regarded as the author of the groups' own publications if no individual person was clearly identified as author. However, the debate continued as to what constituted corporate authorship because, in fact, there is always an individual or group of individuals that actually authors corporate publications. Where to draw the line between personal and corporate authorship could not be determined. Therefore, since the second edition of *Anglo-American Cataloguing Rules* in 1978, corporate bodies are no longer regarded technically as authors, although they can still be considered responsible in various ways for publications. Corporate bodies are the emanators of publications, and only for certain kinds of publications, in certain clearly specified situations, can they be regarded as primarily responsible for the specified publications. Only in such situations can corporate bodies be treated as authors, although they are technically not.

Authorship is not limited to creators of the written word; it also encompasses artists, illustrators, photographers, composers, cartographers, compilers of bibliographies and directories, and others. In AACR2, performers on sound recordings, motion pictures, and video recordings can also be regarded as authors in certain situations.

An unclear area of authorship deals with the creation of new works by a machine, such as a computer. A person (or persons) is responsible for directing the actions of the machine, but the product can be a new work, not previously in existence. In such cases, the copyright principle of works done for hire seems to apply, and the agent owning and directing the machine would be responsible for the final output.

Certain legal and religious works are treated as if the government or religious bodies that issue the works are the authors. Ghost-written works also treat the person who claims to be the author as the author, regardless of his or her actual contribution.

B.1.4.1   Single authorship

An individual person is responsible for creating the content of a bibliographic unit in cases of single authorship. The person may or may not be named specifically in the unit; but if he or she is identifiable, he or she is the author. As pointed out in the preceding section, corporate bodies, in certain closely defined situations, can appear as if they are the authors of their publications, but technically they are not; they are emanating bodies. This distinction arose from the difficulty of defining corporate authorship. In situations where no personal author is named and a corporate body is prominently present in the publication, the publication will be treated as if it has no author unless it can be shown to have emanated from the corporate body and it fits into one of the narrowly defined publication types that indicate that a corporate body is primarily responsible for the publication.

B.1.4.2   Shared authorship

Works of shared authorship are the responsibility of two or more persons or emanate from two or more corporate bodies. In cases of multiple, or joint authorship, the individuals involved have all done the same type of work: written the text or music, created the cartographic item, drawn the illustrations, or performed together, for example. Each person, however, may not have done the same amount of work.

In cases of works produced under editorial direction, various individuals or bodies doing the same kind of activity are brought together by an editor who has them create something new to make up a new work. The individual persons or bodies interact and work together under the direction of the editor, who plans the work and sees it through to completion, but who may not have contributed content to the main body of the work.

Compilations are inherently different from works produced under editorial direction because authors' contributions to a compilation were originally created for some purpose other than that they appear in the compilation. A compiler picks and chooses from various independently created works in order to form a new work. The compiler has no direct influence on the individual authors, unlike an editor. Editors and compilers are not considered to be authors in AACR, though they are responsible for the works they create. Hence, works of shared authorship and compilations are entered under title.

B.1.4.3   Authorship of mixed responsibility

When authorship is that of mixed responsibility, two or more people or bodies have collaborated to produce a new work, but they have each performed different activities doing so. Situations of mixed responsibility occur when an original work has been modified by another person or body, for example, adaptations in any format from one medium to another, illustrations added to written text, work revised by other people, commentary and work published together, reproductions of artworks published with added text, words and music written by different people, and material performed by others. Situations where two or more people create new works are also included, for example, interviews with considerable additions by the interviewer, communications between spirit and medium, writers and illustrators interacting with each other, and academic disputations.

Mixed responsibility does not preclude determining the author with primary responsibility. The author given credit for primary responsibility varies depending on the situation. For example, when illustrations are added to an existing text, the author of the text is primary; if the author and illustrator worked together in producing the work, the name given prominence on the title page is primary. A work revised by another person stays under the original author as long as he or she is indicated as author on the title page; otherwise, the reviser becomes primary.

B.1.4.4   Unknown and diffuse authorship

All works are created by someone, but if the author or authors cannot be identified, the work must be entered under its title. Also, if there is uncertainty as to the author's exact identity, the works are treated as works of unknown authorship. Works emanating from unnamed groups are treated the same. Diffuse authorship occurs when no one of four or more people can be identified as being primarily responsible, or in the case of corporate bodies, no one of four or more bodies can be identified as principal emanator. In such cases, the works are treated the same as works of unknown authorship. A name or names of people or bodies may be associated with the work, but the association is insufficient to indicate primary authorship.

B.1.5   **Formats or types of material**

"Formats" refers to the physical containers, the books or exemplars, of works and texts (see B.1.1). Formats, or types of material, can be divided into various groupings; a traditional one in libraries is that of books, or print, and nonbook, or nonprint or audiovisual. Such a division is unsatisfactory because it lacks precision. The book category generally covers not only the traditional format of the book, but also print serials and other materials. "Nonprint" and "nonbook" are negative terms; they indicate what something is not rather than what it is. Audiovisual is an older term and implies the need for equipment to utilize materials, though there are many types of material that don't need equipment but are usually considered part of this grouping.

There is also apparently little agreement as to what types of material belong in each broad division. Sometimes maps and music scores are regarded as nonbook or nonprint because they obviously are not traditional books, but they are formats that have long been accepted parts of library collections and would generally not be thought of as audiovisual materials. Microformats would seem to be audiovisual in nature because equipment is required for their use, but they usually contain microcopies of print materials, so are often rejected as members of the audiovisual division.

One approach to the problem would be to regard the material's content as more important than its physical container and reject any arrangement by container. But this ignores the different impacts that various formats can make in conveying their content. It would be tempting to classify materials based on impact, but the effects a format will have on the receiver will vary with the person and the circumstances.

Any attempt to arrange materials into some classification based on their physical formats breaks down eventually due to the difficulty of encompassing all the characteristics of the various types. The arrangement that follows is only one possibility and is based on the primacy of text or images and sounds and the need for equipment. Definitions of the specific formats can be found in the *ALA Glossary of Library and Information Science* (1983) and in the glossary of AACR2.

B.1.5.1   Macroforms

Generally, "macroform" is a generic term for any medium that bears images large enough to be easily read or viewed without magnification (see *ALA Glossary*). But a broader approach can be used which would encompass, in addition to books, motion pictures, filmstrips, slides, and other media that require equipment that magnifies or otherwise transforms the content into perceivable images or sounds. In such a context, "microform" would be used exclusively for formats containing optically reduced copies of macroforms (see B.1.5.2).

B.1.5.1.1   No equipment needed

B.1.5.1.1.1   Text

In the category of text-oriented formats requiring no equipment for access are the formats that primarily transmit words, though there may also be illustrations. These include books, pamphlets, technical reports, theses and dissertations, single sheets or broadsides, print serials, wall charts, and many archives and manuscripts. They all carry media-bearing images large enough to be easily read or viewed without magnification.

Pamphlets are arbitrarily included as a subcategory of books, but they are most usefully defined by their purpose rather than their physical format. There is little consensus as to how short a soft-cover book must be to be a pamphlet; therefore, libraries should define pamphlets as any material meant to be used temporarily to meet a current need (see B.3.4.2). Such material is treated differently than are items designated for more permanent homes in the collection. If pamphlets are meant to be kept permanently, they are not treated like other pamphlets.

Print serials are included in the category despite the fact that serials are a pattern of publication, not a format. This is because libraries traditionally bind print serials into booklike physical volumes for permanent keeping. Technical reports frequently are distributed in a microformat, but in their original forms, they are usually distinguished by their content (research results, either ongoing or final), their typescript, and their distribution (through their own dedicated channels).

B.1.5.1.1.2   Nontext

The category of nontext includes the formats that primarily convey symbols and emotions other than words. Included here are cartographic materials, music scores, photographs, technical drawings, three-dimensional objects such as artifacts, realia or specimens and microscope slides, and art originals and reproductions. The photograph format includes the prints made from negatives, since negatives are rarely as accessible as their print copies. Three-dimensional objects could cover any manmade or naturally occurring objects, aside from the other information-carrying formats in section B.1.5, that have been made part of a library collection of bibliographic materials for some purpose. Other formats in section B.1.5 could also become three-dimensional objects if the reason they were incorporated in the collection was to provide an example of the format, not for the information they carry.

B.1.5.1.2   Equipment needed

In the category of formats needing equipment for utilization are formats that require magnification or transposition from one form to another for viewing or listening. These formats include sound recordings, motion pictures, video recordings, filmstrips, slides, transparencies, holograms, and computer files. Filmstrips and slides can be combined with sound recordings (also called audio or phono recordings) to produce new media. Many of these formats encompass variations (see C.7.2): sound recordings and video recordings can be issued on disk or tape; motion picture film can be of varying widths, with or without sound; filmstrips can also vary in width; machine-readable data files (MRDF), or computer files, are probably the most variable in physical format, being contained in many different structures. MRDFs can also be output in a variety of formats with a great range in the kind and complexity of equipment needed for each format.

B.1.5.2   Microforms

Microforms are formats that require equipment that magnifies their images so they can be utilized, but they are limited in content to microreproductions of other text and nontext formats (see B.1.5.1.1.1 and B.1.5.1.1.2), for example, books, print serials, cartographic materials, music scores, and art reproductions. Even some of the formats requiring equipment (see B.1.5.1.2) can be copied in microforms, for example, machine-readable data files, filmstrips, and slides. The reduction used in various microformats can vary, often requiring a variety of lenses for viewing.

All microformats begin as filmed copies; they are then processed into microfilms, microfiches, or microopaques (see C.7.1.1). The size of each final format can vary and may require its own equipment for use.

B.2   Bibliographies and bibliographic control

The term "bibliography" is used to describe all lists of items selected from the bibliographic universe. Such lists can vary greatly as to scope, physical form, arrangement, entry, and bibliographic standards used in compilation. Identifying and locating these items of recorded information, for whatever purpose, and then listing and arranging the descriptions in some order are the elements of bibliographic control. The basic characteristics of a bibliography are as independent of each other as are the characteristics of the bibliographic universe.

It has been common to speak of "analytical" and "enumerative" bibliographies, but these terms do not serve any useful function for categorizing bibliographies. The term "analytical bibliography," which can be divided into three subcategories—historical, textual, and descriptive—is used to cover the history and study of books as physical objects, including their production and the effects of different kinds of manufacturing on their text. "Enumerative bibliography," on the other hand, refers to the listing of books (and by extension, other information-bearing items) according to some system. Enumerative bibliography is the concern of this section.

B.2.1   Bibliographic level

A basic problem in bibliographic control is what unit should be used for listing and describing. A monographic book publication, for example, is frequently divided into chapters, each of which usually has its own title and perhaps even its own author. A print serial commonly consists of individual issues with separate articles, each with its own title and author. A monographic series consists of separate monographic publications that not only can have chapters but also unique titles and authors. Many discrete items in the bibliographic universe can be partitioned into constituent parts or levels, each of which can be separately identified. Each level within a publication that has its own title can form the basis of a bibliographic record.

The size of the listable unit has a profound effect on a bibliography's usefulness and should be made explicit. Many bibliographies do attempt to explain the level of analysis used in their compilation; however, library catalogs rarely do. If more than one level of a bibliographic item is included, a bibliography must link the various levels to make clear the relationship.

B.2.2   Scope

The domain or set of items in the bibliographic universe from which a bibliography's content is selected and drawn defines the outer limits of the scope of a bibliography. Ordinarily, the domain will be larger than the number of items actually listed, as some principle of selection is applied to define and restrict the bibliography's scope. Both the domain and this principle of selection should be clearly explained, but frequently they are not. In order to estimate a bibliography's value, a researcher must know what he or she can expect to find and what the researcher can expect to be excluded. If a bibliography claims to be complete, it is claiming that the scope and domain are identical, that there is nothing in the domain that is not in the bibliography, and that only those items listed meet the requirements for inclusion.

The various elements of scope often overlap and occur simultaneously in each individual bibliography.

B.2.2.1   Purpose

The purpose of a bibliography is to be either comprehensive in relation to its scope, or selective, with its principle of selection clearly stated. A comprehensive bibliography claims it lists all qualified items within its domain; a selective bibliography sets down the limits of the domain, but then, based on some principle, excludes parts of the domain from the selection process. Either purpose is valid as long as it is explicitly stated and followed as closely as possible by the compiler of the bibliography.

B.2.2.2   Period

If a bibliography is "scoped" by period, it attempts to list all items within its scope that are being currently published, were published retrospectively, or are to be published in the future. Bibliographies often combine current and retrospective scopes, but rarely include to-be-published material. To-be-published material is usually gathered in separate bibliographies.

If a bibliography's scope is limited to currently published materials, some definition of "current" must be identified; "within the past year" is common. Frequently, items omitted in previous listings are discovered and included, so current bibliographies may cite some older materials. A retrospective bibliography has to set down the limits of the period it covers: how near to the present does it come and how far into the past does it go? Bibliographies listing to-be-published material are generally limited to material to be published within a certain limited future, but may also list items of indeterminate publication, or even items that never appear. Therefore, the to-be-published scope is the least definite of the three.

B.2.2.3   Coverage

A bibliography is always scoped according to some limit of coverage. Limits of coverage frequently involve more than one element. Coverage may be restricted to the works and manifestations of an author or group of authors sharing some characteristic; such bibliographies also frequently include works about the author or authors, combining author and subject coverage. A bibliography is frequently limited to material on a specific subject; the subject can range from very intensive to quite extensive to any degree in between. The scope of subject coverage is determined by the bibliographer, and any limit is valid as long as the bibliographer makes it explicit.

The place of publication may limit the coverage to one place, several, or many. Such coverage may be further limited by time period. Limiting coverage to works of a particular publisher or group of publishers frequently implicitly limits the place of publication and explicitly limits the time period. If a bibliography is limited by time period, the period can be either the time of publication or the time covered by the content of the listed material. Limitation by language or group of languages can be based on a particular place where the language is predominant or can attempt coverage of all examples of the language wherever it appears.

Bibliographies can be limited by kind of material or format (see B.1.5) or to groups of formats. Scoping by genre limits coverage to one of several varieties of material, usually based on distinctive classes or categories of literary, musical, or artistic composition, such as science fiction stories, symphonies, or abstract art. Basing a bibliography on the elusive scope of quality requires careful definition of the criteria used to determine quality. Several of the most popular criteria are number of copies sold (with the inference that sales reflect quality), selection by a group of experts, and inclusion on lists of most-cited journals.

Bibliographies that include in their coverage contents of printed serials may claim their coverage is cover to cover, that is, all contents of each issue of each serial are listed. This rarely occurs, though, and usually parts of the issues are excluded as being of ephemeral interest only. The excluded parts should be indicated in the bibliography's statement of scope.

B.2.2.4   Function

The function of a bibliography is determined by its intended use. A universal bibliography attempts to list the complete contents of the bibliographic universe with no restrictions. Such a goal may have been possible in the past, but it is no longer considered achievable because the extent of the bibliographic universe is unknown. Compilers of universal bibliographies are striving for complete bibliographic control but are doomed to frustration.

National bibliographies propose to list the publications, usually current, of a particular country. Such bibliographies, however, are often selective, either intentionally or otherwise. Many explicitly exclude certain kinds of material, publishers, genres, and so on. Some also try to include material about the country, so are not limited to national imprints. Trade bibliographies are restricted to the production, usually current, of a country's commercial or trade publishing industry and are published by a trade publisher. Some such publishers may be intentionally or accidentally excluded.

Library catalogs are bibliographies that list materials included in particular library collections and indicate where the material is located. The primary distinction between catalogs and other types of bibliographies is that the idea of location is inherent in catalogs; if an item is listed in a catalog, it is or was at some time part of the collection being indexed by that catalog. Library catalogs appear to be comprehensive for a library's collection but usually intentionally exclude certain kinds of material and even the products of some publishers. The bibliographic level covered in catalogs varies but is frequently limited to the larger unit. Elements of scope and various bibliographic levels rarely are made completely explicit in a catalog; there is usually an incorrect assumption that a catalog is complete for the collection. Union catalogs list the contents of more than one collection and indicate in which collection each item can be found. So-called union lists are actually union catalogs in that the end use of such lists is to indicate the existence and location of the items listed.

Other elements of scope in a library catalog, such as time period and coverage, are determined by the library's collection policies (see B.3.1), which are derived from the goals and objectives of the library's parent institution. In the past, library catalogs could be divided into public catalogs, which were designed for use by the library's public, and official catalogs, consisting of a record for each description (see B.2.5.1) and its access points (see B.2.5.2), the authority files (see B.3.4.1), and the shelflist (see B.3.4.1). Use of official catalogs was restricted to library employees. Such distinctions are disappearing as new forms of catalogs supplant the more traditional ones.

B.2.3   **Physical form**

A bibliography's physical form is dependent on available technology. Since the development of printing, bibliographies in a book or text format—occupying an entire book, part of a book, an entire issue of a print serial, or part of a print serial issue—have been most common. The pattern of publication can be monographic or serial; if serial, periodic, superseding cumulations are common. Even with the development of new printing technologies that greatly shorten the time between compilation and publication, book and print serial bibliographies begin to go out of date as soon as they are set in print. Advantages of the print format, however, are that many descriptions usually appear on a page, making rapid scanning possible, and that complete multiple copies are easily produced.

The use of separate cards, each one containing a discrete description of an item, has been most common for library catalogs, though the cards' use is not limited to such bibliographies. Library catalogs began the change from book format to card format in the last half of the nineteenth century because such a format can be immediately brought up to date by filing new cards at any point in the file. Inherent disadvantages of the card format, though, include the facts that it is difficult to completely duplicate a card file at more than one location, scanning of multiple cards is more difficult than scanning a page in a print bibliography, and card files are more vulnerable to mutilation from heavy use and vandalism. Card files began to be replaced by printed book catalogs around the middle of the twentieth century when new technology made this possible. This new technology, utilizing mechanical data storage and processing equipment (see C.4), and

47

more recently computers manipulating machine-readable databases, is steadily making the card format a thing of the past.

An interim step between the book formats that use new technology and the online format for bibliographies is the microform format. Instead of distributing the bibliography on paper, the data is filmed, reproduced, and distributed in a microformat (see B.1.5.2). It is becoming common to bypass the paper stage completely by putting the information into machine-readable form and then filming it right off a terminal display screen. Such microform bibliographies are called COMs (computer output microfilm). Microform bibliographies are still out of date as soon as they are produced, but the technology allows much more rapid updating and reformatting than in the past, so the lag time is much less than it was previously. Microforms have the advantage over print in that they are cheaper to produce and distribute; their disadvantage is that equipment is needed for utilization.

A newer bibliographic form is the online format. Instead of outputting the machine-readable data file onto paper or microfilm, the data is kept in electronic form and displayed on a terminal upon request. The system's users can request retrieval of all or some of the file, and they usually enjoy more access points and more flexible searching than they would in print, card, and microform formats. Disadvantages to the online format include the need for terminals and the need to instruct people in their use. Many bibliographies now appear only in the online format; however, the print and microform formats may continue to be popular as peripheral supports for the online mode, though the new compact disk format, with its great storage capacity, will probably replace these other formats for this purpose. It is likely that the main bibliographic file will be on compact disk, with records too recent to be entered on the disk available online.

B.2.4   **Arrangement**

Arrangement determines where items of a given type can be found in bibliographies and explains what it means to find an item at a particular place in the list. The number of positions available to which items can be assigned and the rules for assigning items to these positions should be implicitly or explicitly specified in all bibliographies.

Arrangement of all entries (see B.2.5.2.1), including names, titles, and subject access points, in alphabetic order is most common. It is assumed that all potential users know the alphabet; even if they are uncertain about parts of the alphabet, they probably know enough to eventually find their way to where they want to be. But in large files, alphabetic order is usually complicated by special interpretations that create subfiles that no longer follow strict alphabetic order. A further complication is the appearance in bibliographic data of nonalphabetic characters, such as numbers and punctuation. The presence in the file of materials written in non-Roman scripts also must be accommodated. Any variations from straight alphabetic arrangement should be made explicit. Alphabetic arrangement is frequently called dictionary arrangement because most dictionaries are arranged alphabetically in one A–Z alphabet.

Variations of a single alphabetic arrangement are common. If all entries and access points (see B.2.5.2), regardless of type, are arranged in one A–Z alphabet, the arrangement is said to be undivided. If the entries are split into two or more separate and complete alphabets, usually dependent on the type of entry or access point, the file is divided. Such a divided file may have one part containing interfitted author and title access points and another separate part containing the subjects.

The register/index arrangement consists of a register that contains the complete description of all entries arranged in a nonalphabetic order, often that of accession order. Indexes contain the various access points, arranged alphabetically, a brief description of the entry, and an identification number that locates the complete description in the register. Each index is commonly limited to one type of access point.

Serially published cumulated bibliographies commonly merge various issues into a complete new alphabet, superseding the previous issues; the register/index cumulates only the entries in the indexes, while the register is neither cumulated nor superseded.

A classed, or classified, arrangement is based on some classification scheme. Some principle, purpose, interest, or combination of these is used to determine the number and order of the classes into which the bibliographic entries are put (see B.2.5.2.2.2.2). Since the systematic order of the classes is rarely as obvious to users as it is to the classification scheme's creator, and because some users may be seeking known items by title or author, auxiliary alphabetically arranged indexes are usually provided for access to names of subjects, authors, and titles. Since the arrangement of a classed file is not self-evident like the arrangement of an alphabetic file, and because a classed file requires the use of indexes for access, classed arrangements have not been popular for general bibliographies. But a classed arrangement can be a powerful aid in comprehending a subject field's structure and its relation to other fields. Because of this inherent feature of classification, classed arrangement has been most popular in scientific and technical subject areas.

The alphabetico-classed arrangement is similar to an alphabetic arrangement, with the exception of their access points for subjects. In an alphabetic arrangement, access to subjects is direct and specific, that is, the user goes directly to the desired subject with no use of subject subdivision, regardless of its level of specificity. (A work on birds is entered under BIRDS; a work on penguins is entered under PENGUINS.) In

49

an alphabetico-classed arrangement, subjects are grouped into broad generic classes, and access to a specific subject is achieved through successive subdivisions of the broad class in which the specific subject occurs. (Penguins could be found under SCIENCE—ZOOLOGY—VERTEBRATES—BIRDS—PENGUINS.) Subject access in an alphabetico-classed arrangement can be as specific as in an alphabetic arrangement, but access is not direct. A user must know in what chain (see B.2.5.2.2.2.2) the desired specific subject appears; therefore, extensive cross-references are required. Theoretically, the system of alphabetic subject access provided in U.S. catalogs, which is derived from the principles of Charles Ammi Cutter, precludes any elements of the alphabetico-classed arrangement; in fact, American catalogs are rife with such elements.

Other possible arrangements of bibliographic data include chronological arrangements and by-area arrangements. In a chronological arrangement, entries are ordered according to some time sequence. The sequence could be dates of publication, dates of coverage, authors' dates, and so on. Areal arrangement is based on some ordering of the features on the earth's surface or of extraterrestrial worlds. Publications can be grouped by where they were published or by the areas they cover. A well-known areal arrangement is to group all parts of Europe first, followed by Asia, Africa, North and South America, and any place not otherwise covered.

Random arrangement is rarely truly random; frequently, entries are arranged according to the order in which they were added to the bibliography. Such an arrangement requires auxiliary indexes in order for the main descriptions to be retrieved; arrangement in machine-readable data files can be of any kind, but random order, with many indexes, is common.

All bibliographic arrangements, other than alphabetic, usually resort to alphabetic arrangement of entries whenever there is more than one entry in a location. A popular alternative to alphabetic arrangement in groups of entries filed in some subject location is by publication date in reverse order, that is, with the entry published latest listed first.

B.2.5   Bibliographic records

Bibliographic records are the primary components of bibliographies. They should contain the information that uniquely identifies the works and their manifestations that, in the compiler's view, falls within the bibliography's scope. A bibliographic record consists of a description and usually more than one access point that either indicates where the description is located or provides one or more places in the bibliography for the description to be displayed.

B.2.5.1   Description

A description contains all the information elements a compiler judges to be needed to identify the represented bibliographic item. A description is a surrogate for the item itself; it should contain enough information for the bibliography user to determine if the described item is what he or she seeks. The user may wish only to verify the existence of an item; he or she may be seeking a piece of information incorporated in the record and not need to see the item itself; or the user may want the original item and be seeking a clue as to how he or she can obtain it.

The amount of detail in a record can vary, depending on the bibliography's purpose. The amount of information considered sufficient is determined by the compiler, and inclusions and exclusions should be explicitly stated. The record created for library catalogs (see B.2.2.4) has evolved over the years; at present, the necessary information elements and their arrangement is determined by the International Standard Bibliographic Description (ISBD), sponsored by the International Federation of Library Associations and Institutions (IFLA). The *ISBD (G): General International Standard Bibliographic Description* (IFLA, 1977) presents the pattern from which the ISBDs for specific formats and the ISBD for the serial pattern of publication are derived. The various ISBDs are the basis for all the description rules in *Anglo-American Cataloguing Rules*, second edition (ALA, 1978).

A bibliographic record in a library catalog should include the following information elements or areas of description (when they are present in the original item) in the following order:

B.2.5.1.1   Title and statement of responsibility

The first information element will include the item's main title (called the title proper in ISBD) and any secondary titles closely associated with the main title. The original item's format, called general material designation, may also be indicated. The statement of responsibility lists the author or authors (see B.1.4) and the names of people or corporate bodies that made subsidiary contributions (along with their functions) if these names are included in the original item.

B.2.5.1.2   Edition statement and any statement of responsibility unique to one or more editions but not to all editions

Determining different editions can be quite difficult, so heavy reliance is placed on the item's producer when ascertaining a work's variant editions.

B.2.5.1.3   Material-specific information

This area of description contains details required by a specific format (see B.1.5) to describe it thoroughly and is not yet used with all formats. In AACR2, formats that require such information at present are cartographic materials, music scores, computer files, and serially published materials. Other formats may require this area in the future.

B.2.5.1.4   Publication, distribution, etc., information

Traditionally, this information element describes the item's place of publication, the name of the publisher, and the date of publication. Additionally, it may include the place and name of the distributor, the place and name of the printer, and copyright or printing dates.

B.2.5.1.5   Physical description

This element shows the name of an item's specific format and the extent of the item; any additional physical details, such as illustrations, color, or speed; and the physical item's dimensions. If the item is accompanied by other material that is to be used with it, information about this additional material can be included.

B.2.5.1.6   Series statement

If the item is part of a monographic series (see B.1.2.2.1), the collective title of the series will appear next. Any numbering the item has been assigned within the series will be included.

B.2.5.1.7   Notes

Notes include information judged to be necessary or useful in accurately describing the item which could not be included in earlier areas of the description. Notes may explicate some element of the item's physical description, detail some of its bibliographic history, or present information about its content. A convention in library cataloging practice is that no name or title should be made an added entry access point (see B.2.5.2.1) to a description unless it appears somewhere in the description; the notes area can be used to provide the needed justification.

B.2.5.1.8   Standard number and terms of availability

The last ISBD area lists the existing international standard numbering systems and information concerning the price or terms on which the item is available. If the item bears two or more standard numbers of the same kind, brief qualifications are added to explain the presence of more than one number. The only standard numbering systems used at present are the International Standard Book Number (ISBN) and the International Standard Serial Number (ISSN). Both numbering systems are designed to provide unique numbers: the ISBN is assigned to a physical manifestation of a work; the ISSN is assigned to a specific title of a serially published work.

The elements required by the ISBDs and their ordering are necessary only for library catalogs; but most, if not all, of the elements can be found in many other bibliographies that list the largest level of bibliographic items (see B.2.1); and the order is frequently the same. Bibliographies listing smaller units included within the largest level exclude some of the elements, adding instead sufficient descriptive elements of the larger unit so it can be identified. Some bibliographies include greater detail of description, with additional elements, but the basic ISBD areas will usually be present. Tradition, based on usefulness, has determined the necessary elements of a bibliographic description, and future developments probably will not bring many significant changes, though there may be additions.

B.2.5.2   Access points

Access points are added to descriptions and are used to order or arrange (see B.2.4) a bibliography's descriptions and allow them to be searched and identified. Every description must have at least one access point, as it must occupy some location in the bibliography; frequently, however, descriptions have more than one access point. In such cases, the access points contain information and are located in places the bibliographer judges will be helpful to those utilizing the list. The full or partial description may be attached to the access point, or the access point may merely indicate the single location of the full description.

B.2.5.2.1   Entry and heading

The term "entry" is used to denote the actual access points for any bibliographic record. Entry for the description is made under various words or numbers to provide approaches to the record. "Heading" refers to the number of elements in the entry and their order. Heading rules determine what element in the entry comes first, how the following elements are arranged, and whether any elements will be omitted or added to the entry. Heading, therefore, determines the filing of the entry, which is its actual location in the bibliography.

In cataloging parlance, one entry for a record has traditionally been designed as the main entry, other entries are added, and still others are secondary. The concept of main entry derives from the time of early book catalogs when an item's full description appeared only once and was arranged according to the main, most important entry, which was the principal author of the item or the main title if authorship was undetermined. All other item entries contained a brief description and pointed to the main entry for full description. Early card catalogs continued both the distinction between full and brief descriptions and the difference between main and other entries.

As catalog card production evolved, it became common to prepare a full description once, then duplicate it under all entries assigned to the record. The concept of main entry continued, but in a weaker form. The main entry still designated the principal author or the main title entry if no author was known; if the entry cited a principal author, it was the first information item immediately preceding the description at each access point. Other entries were imposed above the main entry for filing purposes. The distinction between main and other entries was no longer important because of any significant differences in fullness of description and probably was transparent to the majority of users. Catalogers were still concerned with the distinction, however, because the cataloging rules, up to and including *Anglo-American Cataloguing Rules*, second edition (ALA, 1978), continued to differentiate between entry types. If the location mark, or call number (see B.3.4.1), for an original item contains a method for alphabetizing the item within its class, the main entry is commonly used for deriving the alphabetizing device; therefore, main entry does continue to have a practical use for this purpose.

But there is another more important use for the concept of main entry, even in online bibliographies where the descriptions are linked to but filed separately from the access points and are displayed together only as the result of a search. A main entry has always been considered to be the most important or the best identification for a record. Traditionally, the main entry consists of the item's author, the name most frequently used to designate the item. Catalogers speak of "title main entry" when entry is made initially under an item's title if there is no discernible author, but, in fact, such a designation is a misnomer. Title main entry really means that there is no main entry and catalogers are falling back on the only element left to arrange the description initially.

Since the main entry is considered to be the primary identifying element, it is useful when an item is referred to in other records. The main entry also performs a vital arrangement function; it brings together under the same entry various manifestations of a work.

The term "added entry" is applied to additional entries made for a record that are derived from actual information found in the record, though the headings may appear in a different form. Secondary entries are added to the record from sources outside the record; examples of secondary entries are subject terms derived from controlled lists and symbols taken from classification schemes.

The actual distinction between entry types is relatively unimportant, with the exception of the main entry. Users' needs vary, so all types of entries must be provided. Though there are bibliographies that satisfy users with just one entry per record, most bibliographies benefit from a multitude of entries, allowing many approaches to the record to meet a variety of needs.

The forms of much nomenclature used as access points can vary over time or can have more than one form at the same time. If the bibliographer wants to use access points as gathering devices, bringing together at one point or under one heading all pertinent descriptions, the entry headings must be controlled, one heading must always be used for an entry, and unacceptable forms must be rejected (see B.2.5.2.2.2). Therefore, provision has to be made for access from the unused forms to the one used as entry. This is done by cross-references, which refer from one heading to another. Cross-references can also be made between different headings that are related in some way.

A collection of controlled headings is called the index vocabulary, which consists of all acceptable terms that will provide direct access to records. Unacceptable terms used as cross-references, together with index vocabulary terms, compose the larger entry vocabulary. The richer the entry vocabulary, the easier it should be for users to locate the records they seek.

A list of controlled terms can be labeled syndetic if it provides such a large entry vocabulary that users can enter the list with almost any term and be led, through references, to the location of the material they seek. It will also contain references that lead to authorized terms that are superordinate, subordinate, or coordinate.

B.2.5.2.2 Types of access points

Entries may be derived, or taken, directly from a record with no change in structure. Examples of such entries include words or key words in the record that are made accessible by a searching medium such as an automated system. Other entries are derived from the record, but the headings are adjusted to conform to the need for a logical arrangement in the bibliography. Still other entries are assigned to the record from sources separate from the record; assigned and adjusted, derived entries are governed by heading rules designed to provide consistency of arrangement.

B.2.5.2.2.1 Derived access points

Derived entries are either taken directly from a record's content with no manipulation by the indexer or are altered in some fashion to conform to the requirements of arrangement. Derived access points are often incorporated into assigned subject heading lists, but the rules for their construction are based on the heading rules for derived entries.

B.2.5.2.2.1.1 Names

Personal names, names of corporate bodies, and geographic names appearing in records can all be made access points for the records. Commonly, these names are manipulated to create headings that will arrange the entries in what is considered to be a useful order. In catalogs, the heading rules are taken from *Anglo-American Cataloguing Rules*, second edition (ALA, 1978); these rules require reordering and addition to or omission of elements in the derived entry.

Personal names are traditionally entered in inverted order, with surname cited first, followed by forename. If the personal name lacks a surname, some other element must be used to arrange the entry. Surnames can have one or multiple elements. A personal name can also vary in fullness, or the individual can be known by more than one name. The name may also need to contain additions, such as dates, titles, or some other designation, in order to make it distinctive.

The names of corporate bodies are usually more complicated than those of persons. Corporate names can be entered in direct order or manipulated to bring some internal element to the fore. Corporate bodies can change their names during their lifetimes, sometimes incidentally, sometimes drastically. They also can be known by different names or forms of the same name at the same time. Corporate bodies frequently have subordinate parts, which often actually author the bibliographic items. Catalogers must decide whether the heading will include or exclude the subordinate body, or even exclude the parent body completely from the heading, and enter directly under the subordinate body. Names of corporate bodies can be nondistinctive and easily confused with other bodies; therefore, some element must often be added to the name to make it unique.

Government agencies create an additional problem for bibliographers who must decide whether the agency should be entered under the government's name or directly under its own name. And the decision to include or exclude elements in a hierarchy of parent and subordinate bodies is a problem with all corporate names, but is particularly acute in government names.

The names of geographic areas have problems similar to those of personal and corporate bodies. Areas change their names, are known by different forms of a name at the same time and over time, can be nondistinctive, and have subordinate or superordinate levels.

Names associated with records are important access points. If headings are manipulated to make them unique, they provide a useful identification of records when users search for known items. But because names can be associated with certain subjects, they can also be used for subject searches. Some persons write only about certain topics; some corporate bodies center their activities in specific subject areas; and some geographic names are associated primarily with particular activities, events, or entities.

B.2.5.2.2.1.2 Titles

Titles are usually derived from bibliographic records and are used as access points with no manipulation, except for the disregarding of initial articles in filing. The part of the main title up to the first significant break can usually be found as an access point. Other parts of the title can also be access points if considered important for retrieval purposes. The title of the monographic series to which an item belongs is also frequently made accessible.

Some works are published in various manifestations (see B.1.1) that may have titles that vary slightly from the original work title or even titles that are completely different. In order to identify the work and link all its manifestations, the concept of uniform title was developed whereby one title is designated as the title of the work and is assigned to each manifestation in addition to the manifestation's actual title. The Bible is an example of a work that requires a uniform title to bring its great variety of versions together. Whether the title proper is the Holy Bible, the New American Student Bible, or the Rainbow Study Bible, all versions are linked under the uniform title: Bible (with added elements drawn from language, version, and part). Access will usually be provided for both the uniform and the actual title, or cross-references will be used to point from the actual title to the assigned uniform title and accompanying description. Series titles may also need manipulation in order to make them distinctive, and uniform titles can be created for them.

B.2.5.2.2.1.3 Numbers

Uniform identifying numbers assigned to records are frequently used as access points. They are derived from outside standard systems, so are unmanipulated when taken from the records. ISBNs and ISSNs (see B.2.5.1) are examples of numbers frequently used as access points. Since they are designed to be unique to an item or to a serial title, they can be expected to retrieve only one or a few related descriptions. Bibliography records also are often assigned sequential numbers that indicate their position in the file. In online bibliographies, these identification numbers can be powerful retrieval devices because each number is unique to a record, but the record must be found before the identification number is apparent.

There are many other systems from which unique numbers can be taken and assigned to bibliographic items. Two well-known examples are the Superintendent of Documents numbering system developed to arrange U.S. government publications, and the various identification numbers assigned to technical report literature. If present in the item, these numbers are usually incorporated into the record and can be used as access points.

B.2.5.2.2.1.4 Key words

Names, titles, and subjects all consist of a word or group of words. If multiword, direct access is commonly provided for only the first significant word; later words are not directly searchable. However, individual words in headings, as well as any word contained in the description, can be access points if the bibliography provides for this; it is a matter of indexing the individual words and linking them to the descriptions.

Searchable individual words in headings and within descriptions are called key words because "key" in computer science denotes a character or characters used to identify a group of data elements, a document, or a record (*ALA Glossary of Library and Information Science*; ALA, 1983, 125). All words can be made accessible, but usually there are certain common words that are excluded; these are put on a stop list, which contains the system's unsearchable words. The ability to search for internal words in headings can aid users locating a specific record when their knowledge of the entries is vague or the headings are complicated. Key words from titles, subject headings, or other parts of the record are also used for subject searching, aiding in the retrieval of records describing items that deal with specific subjects. Since the conventions of bibliographies often prohibit assigning many subject headings to a record because such headings commonly refer to the entire or a major part of the item, the use of key words for subject access can greatly enrich the approach to the records. Subject headings, because they are assigned to records from outside sources, may not describe the subject content in the same way the record does; key words fill in the gaps. Many bibliographies also add abstracts to the records; and access to words in the abstract contributes greatly to such files' usefulness.

Key words are not controlled (see B.2.5.2.2.2) and are derived unaltered from a record's entries, description, and abstract. Key words' uncontrolled nature means that subjects known by various terms are not as easy to retrieve as they would be if only one controlled term was used to describe the subject. The same subject becomes scattered because of variant terminology and the lack of cross-references. But uncontrolled terms are valuable because they do not require the user to know the indexing vocabulary (see B.2.5.2.1) in order to conduct a successful search.

B.2.5.2.2.1.5 Other access points

Other access points that may be provided include places of publication, publisher, distributor or printer name, dates of publication or coverage (either specific dates or a range of dates), type of format, or composition of content. Special formats may also provide entries for such elements as type of musical composition, voices, and instrumentation in music scores and sound recordings; geographic areas, coordinates, and scale for cartographic formats; and type of computer, programming language, and memory needed for machine-readable data files. It seems likely that the trend started by online systems to enrich access to bibliographic records will continue in the future.

B.2.5.2.2.2 Assigned access points

In addition to key words derived from a bibliographic record, an item's subject or subjects are frequently indicated by symbols taken from separate lists or schedules and added to the record. Such symbols may consist of a word or group of words, numbers, or letters or a combination of words, letters, or numbers.

"Subject headings" or "descriptors" are terms commonly applied to lists of alphabetic terms, while "classification" is a term associated with systematic schedules of numbers, letters, or combinations of the two. The lists or schedules contain symbols that are to be assigned to records; only symbols authorized by the lists are to be used; and symbols denoting new or changed subjects are not to be used until they have been authorized by the persons or organizations in charge of the lists or schedules. References are commonly made from unauthorized forms and to related subjects. This controlled vocabulary, as opposed to the uncontrolled vocabulary of derived key words (see B.2.5.2.2.1.4), results in greater consistency and the ability to link all records describing material on the same subject without the scattering that results from the use of key words. A disadvantage of controlled lists is that they may not reflect new terminology and shades of meaning as well as key word systems. Applying controlled lists is also more time consuming and requires intellectual effort, which key word systems avoid.

A bibliography's ability to allow retrieval of all material it contains on a desired subject is called recall, while its ability to allow retrieval of only material on the subject, and no other material, is called precision. Recall and precision are used as measures of the effectiveness of access provided by a bibliography, but both measures are difficult to compute. The recall ratio, or ratio of records retrieved to the number of pertinent records in the file, which determines the completeness of a search, could be found by looking at each item represented by the bibliography, then testing the system with searches; but many bibliographies are too large to do this. The precision ratio, or ratio of pertinent records retrieved to the total number of records retrieved, which determines the efficiency of a search, is judged by independent evaluations of pertinence, which can vary over time and according to evaluative method and experimenter. By their nature, recall and precision work in opposition to each other; when one is high, the other tends to be low.

Subjects are related to each other in various ways. There are broad topics that subsume less general topics, and subjects of the same comprehensiveness that are related to each other through specific characteristics or aspects. It should be possible to take lists of subject terms and chart their relationships, both from the general to the specific and vice versa, and between subjects of equal rank in the same and other hierarchies. A particular topic could be described by the name of the family of which it is a part, by topics on other levels of its hierarchy, or by a term that specifically denotes the topic, excluding all other topics or parts of topics. Some lists provide great specificity, allowing identification of minute topics, while other lists provide only general levels, allowing limited specificity. The amount of specificity provided by a subject system affects that system's search precision. The greater a topic's specificity, the more precise the search can be. If there is no way to link related specific topics and search on the larger group by moving up the hierarchy, however, recall will probably be lowered.

Exhaustivity refers to the way bibliographic materials are analyzed for subject content. If only an item's comprehensive subjects are indicated, then a searcher will be unable to access subjects dealt with in smaller units or lower levels of the items (see B.2.1), and recall of these smaller subjects will be impossible. If, however, subject terms are used to bring out the content of, for example, book chapters or serial articles, then indexing is more exhaustive, and recall will be improved. Precision will probably be lowered, however, as more records will be retrieved, increasing the possibility that there will be records judged not pertinent. How exhaustively a subject system is applied is a decision of the bibliography's manager, though lack of specificity in the system would preclude much exhaustive analysis. Exhaustive analysis is expensive because it takes time and effort, and the end result may not justify the means.

Bibliographic subject analysis systems have traditionally been based on the material being described, rather than on purely theoretical principles. Usually a subject does not exist in the system until it has appeared in some item that the bibliography will describe. An existing subject changes its name or its relation to other subjects only when the literature indicates such a change. This driving force behind subject systems is called literary warrant: The existence of literature (in any format, pattern of publication, and so on) sufficiently warrants the existence of a subject that is to be added to the scheme. In reality, few schemes can react so quickly; when a subject first appears in bibliographic material, there are often questions about its correct name and its correct place in the existing system. Therefore, there is usually a time lag before new subjects are added, enabling more material to appear and provide information about the subject and support for its existence. Key word systems, on the other hand, appropriate terms as soon as they appear in the records.

Some subject systems try to provide the names of all subjects encompassed within the scope of the list. General and specific topics are listed, along with necessary cross-references. Some specified groups of names are commonly excluded, such as most personal, corporate, and geographic names and names of members of some large topics, but the list's instructions allow them to be used as needed. Such schemes are labeled enumerative, as they are attempts to enumerate, or list, all applicable topics on all allowable levels. *Library of Congress Subject Headings* is an example of a widely used enumerative list. Synthetic systems, on the other hand, enumerate far fewer topics but provide instructions for joining together listed topics to create terms for composite subjects. (The Colon Classification (CC) is an example of such a synthetic system.) Typically, synthetic systems are much less extensive than enumerative systems and have detailed instructions for forming new subjects. They have the ability to react more quickly to the appearance of new composite subjects and are more flexible than enumerative schemes because parts of new subjects already exist and can be assembled into new terms when needed, rather than waiting until the scheme's manager decides to enumerate them. A disadvantage of synthetic schemes is that they require more instructions and practice to be used successfully; and their application by different individuals may not be as consistent as the application of enumerative schemes, which require less judgment on the indexer's part.

The parts of a synthetic scheme can be analyzed and grouped into fundamental concepts, or facets, the members of which share common characteristics. One possible basis for faceting is to divide all subjects into things; kinds of things; parts of things; material from which things, kinds, or parts are made; properties of things, kinds, parts, or materials; operations upon things, kinds, parts, or materials; and agents performing such operations (*Dewey Decimal Classification,* 19th ed.; 1979, v.1, xlix). Synthetic schemes that are initially developed using faceting principles are called faceted. Faceting procedures are being used in older synthetic schemes as well and are even showing up in enumerative schemes. Faceting provides more consistency and predictability in subject arrangement and reveals relationships otherwise invisible. A notation is often provided that makes relationships explicit.

PRECIS (Preserved Context Indexing System) was developed by Derek Austin for the British National Bibliography when it changed to automated procedures. PRECIS is a set of rules for creating index terms. The terms are arranged in an order specified by the PRECIS rules so the chain of terms may be rotated (or shunted) to make each significant term an access point with no loss of meaning. When terms are first used, they are put into a list of previously authorized terms, and the accompanying reference structure is added. So PRECIS is neither enumerative, since the terms are created as needed, nor synthetic, as there are no previously determined broad concepts to be combined as needed to express more specific concepts.

Many subjects can be described only by combining more than one concept in the name or symbol denoting the subject. Such multitopic subjects combine two or more simple subjects in order to describe another frequently more specific subject. An example of such a multitopic subject is academic libraries, which combines two less specific subjects, academe and libraries, to create a more specific, narrower topic. If topics are correlated or coordinated at the time of indexing, and assigned in their linked form to a record, they are said to be precoordinated; and systems that contain such linked terms are called precoordinate indexing systems.

One problem with precoordinate systems is the lack of consistent rules for determining the order in which terms will be linked; such rules are needed so that new terms will be compatible with existing ones, and so that a searcher can predict with some confidence where to find multitopic subjects. Access to terms not in a multielement subject's lead position should also be made, usually through cross-references; unfortunately, this is not always done consistently. The advantage of precoordinate systems is that subjects can be specified precisely because of the use of multiple elements, and only records describing material containing that precise assigned subject will be retrieved when searched. Precision is helped, but probably at the expense of recall.

If multiple elements are not coordinated at the time of indexing, but instead records containing composite subjects are assigned single-concept terms for each part of the subject, then the single concepts could be combined later at the time of searching. Systems designed to be coordinated at the time of searching are called postcoordinate indexing systems. Such systems allow access on all parts of the multiple-topic subject, and users need not be concerned with the combined elements' order until the search stage. Elements can be combined at the search stage by asking that two or more terms occur simultaneously in the same records (Boolean *and*), that two or more terms occur in records but not necessarily in the same records (Boolean *or*), or that terms occur in records but not in records that contain certain other terms (Boolean *but not*).

A disadvantage of postcoordinate systems is that the retrieved records may not be on the desired subject because the terms have linked in an inappropriate manner during the search. For example, a search using the terms "school" and "library" would retrieve material on school library and library school if the conjunction *and* were used; but if *or* were used, material on many other aspects of schools and libraries would also be retrieved. Due to this possibility of false coordination, elements of precoordination are frequently present in postcoordinate systems. Recall tends to be enhanced in postcoordinate systems, though precision will probably decline.

B.2.5.2.2.2.1 Subject headings and descriptors

"Subject headings" is the term commonly applied to lists of terms found in precoordinate systems, while "descriptors" is applied to topics in postcoordinate systems. Both refer to alphabetic terms, which are used to denote subjects. Their vocabulary is controlled, references from unacceptable terms are provided, and elements of hierarchy are represented by references to narrower, broader, and coordinate terms. Subject heading lists are commonly used in library catalogs, while descriptors, contained in lists called thesauri, are generally used in indexes to microlevel material, such as periodical articles, technical reports, and book chapters. Thesauri usually contain systematic attempts to reveal the logical order among terms, while subject heading lists usually fail to do this consistently.

Two important features of alphabetic terms are semantics and syntax. "Semantics" refers to the meaning of words: it is manifested by the selection of a certain term or group of terms to describe a specific subject and the exclusion of other terms. Many subjects can be described by a variety of terms in a variety of combinations; however, in controlled lists, only one term or group of terms should denote a particular subject. The remaining terms or groups would then become references pointing to the accepted name of the subject. Terms that are applied to various aspects of a subject or that indicate shades of meaning may all be subsumed under one selected name.

"Syntax" refers to the way words are combined to form subject names. Rules of syntax determine the order of terms in a string and which term comes first in succession, making it directly accessible. Semantics is important in both pre- and postcoordinate systems because it governs the choice of terms. Syntax becomes important when two or more terms are linked together and is therefore an important feature of precoordinate systems.

Typically, the best subject name is either the plural or singular form of a single noun. If both forms are used in the same system, one form may connote the general or abstract, and the other may connote specific aspects or things (for example, THEATER used for the art; THEATERS used for the structure). But many subjects may take only compound terms (for example, INTERNATIONAL RELATIONS, INFORMATION STORAGE AND RETRIEVAL SYSTEMS). Compound terms may consist of two nouns joined by a connective, a noun with a modifying adjective in direct or inverted order, or even complex phrase headings. Any combination of two or more terms raises syntax problems. In many alphabetic subject systems, subdivisions showing format, noncomprehensive treatment, special aspects, or chronology are provided and can be added to subjects in various situations; these also raise questions concerning syntax.

B.2.5.2.2.2.2 Classification

Bibliographic classification systems contain classes of subject names arranged in a systematic order, according to some principle or purpose. Each subject class is based on some characteristic that is common to all members of the class and that excludes all nonmembers. A hierarchy of classes, in which each class term includes all those terms that are subsumed in it, is called a chain. Groups of coordinate classes formed by subdividing a more general class according to a particular characteristic are called arrays. The ordered succession of chains and arrays, with included subject names, constitutes the classification schedule. The schedule's structure is derived from a conception of the "correct" order of things, an order that system users will find useful and familiar. In the past, classification systems were frequently created by persons who each believed that his or her own system of classes (number and order) was the most nearly correct and reflected the true order of things in nature. However, since each person's system was functional, it appears that attempts to find an inerrant order are questionable.

To class order is added notation, a system of symbols, usually letters, numbers, or a combination of both, that is used as a form of shorthand to represent the schedule's divisions. Notation substitutes for class names when the classification is applied to a bibliography's records or to the bibliographic material itself for purposes of arrangement on shelves. In synthetic classification systems, notation from different classes and from tables of common subdivisions can be combined to provide precise specification of composite subjects. However, an order of precedence in which these elements are combined must be provided. Such orders of precedence are called citation, or combination, order.

In order to apply the classification schedule and derive the correct notation, users must know in which classes subjects have been placed. The schedule provides an order of classes that may not be obvious to the user, even though cross-references may be present. Therefore, an index to the subjects, in alphabetic order, is usually provided. If the classes in the classification schedule are arranged initially into broad disciplines, the index will also show the disciplines in which a subject can be placed. Such indexes are called relative indexes.

The schedule, notation, and index constitute the classification system. In addition, there must be provided some way of adding new subjects and attendant notation to the schedules, as well as some way of changing class relationships when literary warrant requires. If a classification system is not kept up to date and fails to reflect current literature being added to the bibliography, it will eventually fall into disuse.

B.2.6   Bibliographic standards

Even if a bibliography is compiled by only one individual and is to be a solitary effort with no later additions, bibliographic standards would still be important because assumedly the bibliography was created to be used by others. Bibliographers must observe accepted standards in describing bibliographic materials, providing access to the records, and arranging the records if bibliographies are to be useful.

There are a variety of standards used to compile bibliographies. *Anglo-American Cataloguing Rules,* second edition (ALA, 1978) is considered the standard for description and for access points in library catalogs, but other standards are in use with other bibliographies. Standard numbering systems such as ISBN and ISSN are increasingly used in bibliographies of all kinds, but there are many other numbering systems also in use. Subject specification is provided through many subject heading and descriptor schemes and by a variety of classification systems. Online systems require a whole new set of standards. Only when there is alphabetic arrangement is there unquestioned agreement as to the standard elements and order, but this applies only if all systems use the same alphabet. Even bibliographies of similar scope, format, or arrangement will use different standards for various features. This plethora of standards forces bibliography users to be flexible, lest they become confused and discouraged.

No overseeing body currently imposes consistency in all bibliographic standards, nor is it generally agreed that there should be such an organization. Few bibliographers wish to give up their autonomy in deciding what methods best suit their purposes. But at a minimum, bibliographic standards should be explicit and easily understood. If it were possible to meld all existing bibliographies into one huge entity, then the need for bibliographic standardization would become paramount, and agreement would have to be reached. Currently, there is increasing cooperation in the creation and maintenance of automated bibliographic databases, resulting in an increased awareness of the importance of standards and interest in their development.

The National Information Standards Organization (NISO) Z39 is the United States nongovernment body that promulgates bibliographic standards. Most U.S. agencies involved with bibliographic materials, records, and dissemination belong to NISO, but adherence to its standards is voluntary, and there are still areas of bibliographic control unaddressed by Z39 committees. However, many organizations doing bibliographic work try to observe published standards, and there is much activity to create more.

B.3   Library processes

Libraries and information centers contain bibliographic materials, provide access to such materials, and supply services derived from these materials. These services are usually not based solely on materials actually present in a library's collection, but increasingly are enriched by access to materials in other collections. Wherever the collections of bibliographic materials are, certain procedures or processes are performed to create such collections, ensure their continual usefulness, and provide for their exploitation. These processes have been common to bibliographic collections for a long time, though the methods used to execute them may have changed. The order in which these processes are performed is not always the same in all libraries, so the following arrangement is not necessarily linear.

B.3.1   **Collection management**

The concept of collection development, or materials acquisition, has been evolving recently to that of collection control, or collection management. This concept encompasses the design of a process for selecting bibliographic materials to meet a library's needs, goals, objectives, and priorities. Academic libraries, more often than ever, are establishing levels of collection development. Subject areas in which a library collects are each assigned levels of intensity to be collected, determined by the users' curricula and research interests. Systems of levels of co-operative collection development have been developed by the Association of Research Libraries, the Research Libraries Group, and the American Library Association. Collection development levels for libraries in an entire region were developed, implemented, and measured by the Pacific Northwest Library Association with the support of the Fred Meyer Foundation in a project called LIRN (Library and Information Resources of the Northwest).

Collection management also includes the processes of making materials accessible and of analyzing materials to see if they meet the goals and objectives of a library and its users. Collection management requires a collection development policy that is constantly refined through continual collection analysis. A major part of this planning process is periodic evaluation of how well a collection meets users' and potential users' needs.

Evaluating a collection's usefulness can be done in many ways. Quantitative methods include compiling and analyzing statistics on circulation, counting a collection's materials, determining how much has been and is being spent to develop collections, direct observation of use, citation analysis, and checking holdings against standard bibliographies. Qualitative assumptions are based on these quantitative measures. Surveys of a collection's users and potential users, either by questionnaires or interviews, could also reveal useful information, as can the application of external standards developed by such agencies as the American Library Association and its divisions and by subject specialists or consultants.

A major function of a collection development plan is to identify procedures for acquiring new materials. The plan should also help allocate the budget to meet various needs and establish policies for reviewing and modifying the plan to meet changing needs. Storage, weeding, and preservation policies also need to be established as part of collection management. A thorough plan includes all procedures affecting the maintenance and accessibility of materials after they are acquired. This requires that the collection development plan be coordinated with other library processes, such as cataloging, circulation, interlibrary loan, binding, security, storage, and preservation.

Because services are usually not dependent solely on a library's internal collections but rely also on materials foreign to the library, a collection development plan must take these external collections into account. Reliance on other collections to serve a library's own users' needs can be formalized through cooperative plans such as resource sharing agreements. Resource sharing is based on the assumption of equivalency: libraries receive as much as they give. A library can rely on another's collection to help meet some of its own needs, but it should also help provide for the other's needs with materials from its own collections. In order for such agreements to work, all participants must know what each has and will be acquiring in the future; preparing collection inventories, including collection development levels in various subject areas, to be shared by all libraries party to the agreement, is a common method.

The Research Libraries Group Conspectus was developed to facilitate the process of cooperative collection development. All participants consent to provide an agreed-upon level of service to each other whenever required. Resource sharing agreements can greatly enrich the material-based services available to a library's publics, as well as rationalize the selection process by allowing the library to concentrate on limited subject areas, confident that other areas are being covered in depth by other members of the agreement. Different levels of collection intensity can be assigned by subject, based on knowledge of one's own and other libraries' selection policies.

B.3.2   **Acquisitions**

The acquisitions process encompasses the procurement of bibliographic materials by purchase, exchange, or gift. It includes preorder searching, ordering and receiving materials, processing invoices for payment, and keeping necessary records.

Purchases can be made directly from publishers or producers or through intermediaries such as subscription agents, book jobbers or wholesalers, auction houses, or book dealers. Acquiring library materials can be done individually, piece by piece, or through automatic predetermined selection methods such as approval plans. The parameters of approval plans are determined by a library's collection development process (see B.3.1) in consultation with the wholesaler, jobber, or publisher. Materials conforming to the parameters or profile are automatically sent to the library for review; return privileges are granted.

Purchased material also includes materials received automatically as a result of memberships in societies and associations.

Other automatic acquisitions plans include standing orders and blanket orders. Standing orders are used primarily for acquiring monographic series (see B.1.2.2.1). The library places an order for all titles in the series, which are sent and paid for as they are published. The order stands as long as the series continues or is canceled by the library. Libraries can also place standing orders for the parts of a multipart monographic publication as they appear or for specified types of publications from selected publishers.

Blanket orders are plans under which a publisher or wholesaler supplies all publications defined by the plan, generally at a considerable price reduction and without return privileges. An example of such a plan is a blanket order for all publications of certain university presses. Another example is the Greenaway Plan, which is a blanket order plan developed for public libraries whereby libraries receive at a lower cost advanced copies of trade titles so they can select those titles they want to order in multiple copies.

There are two kinds of materials exchanges: direct and duplicate. Direct exchanges occur when a library sends specified materials to another library in exchange for materials of similar value. A library may run its own exchanges or exchanges may be handled elsewhere in the parent institution. Materials to be exchanged may have been purchased by the library or published by it or other units in its institution.

Duplicate exchanges occur when a library makes its duplicate, unwanted materials available to other libraries in exchange for their duplicates. Costly in terms of personnel time for sorting, storing, listing, mailing, and checking received lists, exchange materials should have no additional acquisitions costs, except perhaps for mailing charges. Materials received through duplicate exchange are sometimes unpredictable but occasionally yield anxiously sought items. Direct exchange may be the only way to acquire certain materials, particularly from some foreign countries. Though the personnel cost as well as the value of exchanges, particularly duplicate exchanges, has been questioned in the past, both exchanges continue to flourish.

Gift materials can arrive unsolicited or be actively encouraged by a library. Usually gifts arrive as single or several items, but they could also consist of fairly large quantities of material collected by someone and then donated as a coherent collection. Soliciting desirable gift collections, for example, rare book collections, can be a major library activity.

A depository agreement between a library and a government that results in the library receiving all or a selection of the government's current publications on a regular basis can be regarded as a type of gift. It differs from other gifts, however, in that the agreement requires the library to process, organize, and make available the government publications on an equal level with the rest of its collections. Also, the materials may not be discarded without the approval of their source.

Some countries require that copies of publications be deposited at a specified location as a condition for copyright protection; therefore, the library receiving the deposits acquires many of the materials it needs without purchase. Such copyright deposits, however, necessitate record keeping in order to support the requirements of copyright.

B.3.3
Processing

Processing covers all activities necessary to physically prepare bibliographic materials for circulation, excluding those functions performed in the acquisitions (see B.3.2) and organization (see B.3.4) processes. Accessioning is the procedure through which a library takes physical custody of bibliographic materials. In the past, this often consisted of recording new acquisitions in a separate accession record and assigning each item a unique accession, or identification, number based on its order of arrival. The materials' sources might also be recorded and ownership marks applied. Now accessioning most monographic items is likely to be confined to adding ownership marks. Check-in is the procedure libraries use to take possession of serially published items and perhaps also of multipart monographic publications. A check-in record is used to record the receipt of each part of the item, and the new part is ownership marked and identified with a call number (see B.3.4.1). Usually libraries also record the date of receipt.

Preparing materials for use can be termed "finishing." This covers the addition of details needed for an item's circulation, such as circulation slips, pockets, machine-readable labels, and so on. Libraries also add ownership marks if not already affixed. Finishing also covers any mending needed to get materials ready for use or to keep materials in condition for continued use. Library binding covers the methods used to permanently hold together the content of bibliographic items and provide them with hard-cover protection for prolonged use. It may consist of rebinding previously bound items, binding separate, unbound parts together in one physical volume, or binding separate units that previously lacked hard covers. Library binding can be done within the library or the library's parent institution, but materials are more likely sent out to a commercial library binder for processing. Mending and other finishing will often be done in-house.

B.3.4
Organization

Bibliographic materials have to be organized for use by a library's publics. An important part of organization is preparing bibliographic records that conveniently describe and represent the materials themselves (see B.2.5). The records are then organized and made available for use; and the material itself is labeled so it can be stored. Therefore, organi-

69

zation consists of preparing bibliographic records, arranging them in catalogs (see B.2.2.4), and placing the actual materials on shelves in a predetermined, useful order. These processes are commonly grouped together and labeled cataloging, but there are also many variations of these traditional activities of cataloging.

B.3.4.1   Cataloging

One of cataloging's traditional processes is the preparation of bibliographic records, which entails recording descriptions and determining all points of access to the record (see B.2.5.1 and B.2.5.2). Recently, automation has greatly impacted the preparation of bibliographic records. The development of the MARC (Machine-Readable Cataloging) formats for recording bibliographic data and transmitting it from one library to another has increased information sharing and reduced the need for each library to prepare original cataloging for the materials it acquires. MARC data for many of the bibliographic materials held in libraries are now available from other libraries and distributed through bibliographic networks (see A.3.1 and A.3.2) to any subscribing library. MARC's high standard of cataloging meets most libraries' needs.

A classification number, representing the subject content, is frequently assigned to a bibliographic item so the item can be organized within the collection (see B.2.5.2.2.2.2). Often added to the classification number is another element consisting of a set of numbers or letters derived from the record's main entry (see B.2.5.2.1); these two elements together create a unique identifier called the call number. Call numbers are used to arrange materials in some useful sequence, which not only indicates subject content but also relationships among subjects. Call numbers also uniquely identify an item in a specific collection so the item can be recorded and retrieved. Files of copies of bibliographic records arranged by call number are called shelflists and are used for inventory purposes. Shelflists frequently contain the most accurate and current information about number of copies and volumes.

Access points attached to bibliographic records should be under authority control, which includes determining the authoritative forms for all adjusted derived headings (see B.2.5.2.2.1) and assigned headings (see B.2.5.2.2.2) in the catalog and adding any appropriate cross-references to the headings. This prevents variant forms of names, subjects, and uniform titles from being authorized for use, which could result in the scattering of related records and the failure to relate works and their books (see B.1.1). If variant forms of headings are used, without authority control, users may not receive full and accurate information about the library's actual holdings. Authorized forms with references constitute an entry vocabulary (see B.2.5.2.1) of controlled terms for the catalog.

Libraries that share cataloging records generally agree beforehand to follow the conventions of specified sets of rules and controlled lists. In some organizations, such as the Online Computer Library Center (OCLC), this agreement is voluntary; in others, such as the Western Library Network (WLN), agreement is monitored by the central staff, and only authorized access points are permitted into the authority file.

Whenever a heading's authorized form has to be changed, its appearance in all bibliographic records must also be changed. In manual catalogs, this revision can be quite difficult, but in automated catalogs, it is possible to strip the headings from the bibliographic descriptions and store the headings in separate files with links to the parent description. This linkage allows a heading to be changed in one place, resulting in changes in all linked records. Such automated authority control is a vast improvement over manual systems, but intellectual effort is still required to solve problems of matching, of whether or not a change has occurred, the preparation of references, and so on.

Libraries can convert existing manual records to machine-readable form so they can become part of the automated catalog (usually called the online public access catalog (OPAC)), even though more than ever such catalogs appear on compact disk (see B.2.3 and C.5.2.1.3.2.3). However, this conversion is difficult because of the need to reconcile headings created under old rules and early editions of controlled lists with current practice. The increase in this conversion process, often called retrospective conversion, or RECON, has revealed problems caused by the lack of authority control in the past and has greatly encouraged its development now.

After a library prepares bibliographic records, it arranges them in catalogs (see B.2.2.4), which have to be managed. Catalog maintenance consists of determining the physical form and arrangement of the catalog; planning for future needs; arranging for records to be added, corrected, and deleted; and providing help to catalog users through instructions, guides, and personal assistance.

B.3.4.2 Other methods of organization

Materials in some formats (see B.1.5) are organized differently than books and print serials, to which traditional cataloging procedures are applied. The reasons for this appear to be based on the assumption that the expected use of such formats will either be enhanced by such treatment or will not be affected too badly if libraries use less expensive cataloging methods.

Pamphlets (see B.1.5.1.1.1) are thought to have only ephemeral value, so full cataloging would be too expensive for their worth and would delay their accessibility past the point of their greatest usefulness. Therefore, pamphlet materials are frequently arranged in folders in vertical file cabinets, and access is provided only to each folder's broad subject area. Their subject access points may be incorporated in the catalog with reference to the vertical file. Libraries' vertical files are frequently underused because neither library staff nor the public is very familiar with their existence or contents.

Some formats have regular bibliographic records prepared, but materials are arranged in accession number order (see B.3.3) to avoid the effort and expense of classification. Such an ordering does make it easier to select more current materials, but provides no subject access. Audiovisual materials (see B.1.5) frequently have been arranged in this fashion.

Archives—organized, noncurrent records resulting from the transactions of the affairs of corporate bodies or persons and preserved because of their continuing value (the *ALA Glossary of Library and Information Science* (ALA, 1983))—are arranged according to the principle of provenance; that is, records of an originating body or person are kept together, usually in the order imposed on them by their creator. Traditional library methods of description and access are not used, but instead names derived from the records become the major points of access.

Publications originating from the U.S. federal government (see B.1.3.1) are frequently organized according to the Superintendent of Documents classification scheme, which is a scheme based on source, not subject. This classification cannot be integrated with the classification used for nongovernment materials, so these materials are segregated in the collection by their source. They also are rarely fully cataloged, but instead identification of items and access to them is provided by bibliographies other than the library's catalog. The library may also incorporate the publications of other governments into such an organization.

Technical reports (see B.1.5.1.1.1) are often arranged by report series, then by report code number within the series. Bibliographies separate from the library's catalog most often supply access to this material.

Other formats that frequently require special treatment are maps, arranged by area and accessible through index maps; and sound recordings, arranged by manufacturers' identification numbers. Rare or special materials, usually defined by market value, may be arranged in any order thought to be useful to the user, such as grouping together miniatures, items with fore-edge paintings, materials with exceptional bindings, or materials acquired by or associated with a particular individual. Bibliographic access to rare materials is frequently expanded in order to reduce the users' need to handle the actual items.

Libraries also have developed other types of organizations to meet specific needs. For example, some libraries arrange their English-language fiction alphabetically by main entry with classification numbers only implied. This fiction may be further segregated into certain genres, such as mysteries, science fiction, romances, and westerns. Libraries commonly keep materials written for children or young adults separate from materials aimed at adults and may further arrange it to meet user needs. There can also be items that have been assigned regular call numbers but that are transferred to some temporary organization to meet readers' short-term interests or because they are needed for an exhibit or display. Materials in reference collections are given regular call numbers but are permanently assigned to a location apart from the regular organization. Collections of separate materials temporarily reserved for special use, such as in reserve rooms (see B.3.6), are also common in some libraries.

B.3.5 **Storage**

Formats of bibliographic materials usually determine the materials' storage. Materials with a book-like shape are stored upright on shelves with labeled spines outward if the items' size permits. Formats that are not book-like can be put into book-like receptacles and intershelved with other book materials. Such treatment can also be applied to many nontext (see B.1.5.1.1.2), equipment-needed (see B.1.5.1.2), and microform (see B.1.5.2) formats to provide equal physical access with that of text formats (see B.1.5.1.1.1) and to enhance use. Converting audiovisual formats into a pseudoprint format, however, is an expensive use of space and packaging materials and may cause damage to the items.

Other formats should be stored differently for best results. Maps should be kept flat, either in large drawers or on hangers, so they won't disintegrate along the folds. Slides need protective storage to discourage fingerprints and dust; they also require some method of displaying them for selection. Machine-readable data files and video recordings need protection from magnetic disruption. And photographs require special storage facilities, as do three-dimensional objects.

All bibliographic formats can benefit from storage especially designed to preserve them as long as possible, but such storage often conflicts with the library's need to provide users with easy and equal physical access to materials. Therefore, a tension exists between the requirements of preservation (see B.3.9) and the requirements of access. Greater physical access results in greater use, but will probably result in faster deterioration of the materials. A library's goals and objectives must address this conflict and resolve it to the benefit of its publics.

Library shelving can be open (users are given direct access to material on the shelves); closed (users are not allowed access to the shelves but instead must request materials through library personnel); or mixed (a combination of closed and open shelves for different users). Material assumed to be most in demand is made directly accessible, while less-used materials are removed from direct access and stored in closed areas. Open shelving is most expensive because materials must be shelved in some useful order, such as by classification number, and materials must be removed easily and easily replaced in the correct sequence. Continual maintenance of the shelving order is required, as is planning for the future so new materials can be intershelved in the correct order. The shelving area's environment must be adjusted to meet users' needs, which is not always the same as the environment required by bibliographic materials. But open shelving does facilitate browsing, which can be a powerful addition to the access provided by catalogs.

Closed shelving can be designed primarily with the physical characteristics of materials in mind. Library personnel do not need to maintain a classified order but can instead install a more efficient and much less costly arrangement by size and accession number. Compact storage is an area of shelving in which bookcase sections are designed to provide the greatest possible shelf capacity through narrower aisles and adjustable shelves. It even can consist of motorized movable bookcases that are stored against each other with no aisles until access to a particular shelf is required. Compact storage can be open but is more often closed; it is frequently utilized for less-used materials. Closed shelving precludes browsing, which could hinder use.

Library materials can be stored in the library or at a remote location. Less-used materials are usually stored at remote locations when space in the library becomes scarce and has to be reserved for items in greater demand. Remote storage facilities may be used by only one library or by a group of libraries sharing the space. Access to such collections is indirect; a user identifies an item in the catalog and it is delivered from the remote facility on a predetermined schedule. Physical accessibility is hindered, but such less expensive storage probably is the only way for many libraries to economically retain such materials. Other libraries may discard such less-used materials in order to save their in-house storage capacity for more useful items.

A newer way to store bibliographic materials is to store their content in machine-readable forms and access them online; the original physical format is destroyed but the content is preserved. Not only is the space required to store materials greatly reduced but online systems provide rapid and enhanced access to their contents. An item's content can then be printed out in hard-copy format if the user desires. Contents can be kept in computer storage or loaded on optical disk and retrieved as needed at any location that has the required output equipment. Because online and optical disk storage require the use of machines to access the contents, this may bar browsing of collections.

B.3.6 **Circulation or use**

Library materials are acquired in order to be used. In-house, or in-library, use is a major factor in the exploitation of many materials and can be difficult to measure accurately. Some categories of materials, such as reference collections, are usually restricted to in-house use because they are in continual demand. Rare materials are restricted because of their value. Some libraries restrict use of their entire collections to in-house use, though most allow the majority of their holdings to circulate outside the library. Circulation requires an accurate record of what is circulating, to whom, and how long that person can use the materials outside the library. Circulation periods vary depending on the type of material to be circulated or even the status of borrowers. Call numbers (see B.3.4.1) are one way to identify individual items; however, machine-readable labels containing identification numbers and affixed to the item frequently are being used instead. Authorized borrowers are registered by a library and given identity cards so they can check out materials. Circulation routines are increasingly being automated to control more efficiently check-out, borrowers' records, and the claiming required for overdue materials (see also C.8.2).

Reserve collections are collections of material kept apart, usually temporarily, from the main collections and assigned limited loan periods so the materials will be more available to groups that have a special need for them. The materials may be restricted so that they can be used only in-house, though some reserve collections do allow items to circulate outside the library for a brief period. Reserve collections are common in school and academic libraries where the requirements of class readings and assignments make sharing limited materials imperative. Public libraries may also have temporary reserved collections that circulate at special locations, such as retirement homes, prisons, and hospitals.

Because libraries often must use other libraries' collections to meet their own users' needs, some formal way of borrowing outside collections is necessary. Therefore, interlibrary loan procedures are common in libraries; an item is identified, its probable location ascertained, and a formal request prepared and sent to the owning library. The borrowing library agrees to certain requirements if the item is loaned. The borrowing library monitors the item's use and returns it to the owning library. Now that bibliographic networks contain extensive holdings information, exact locations of needed items are usually known before requests are sent. Interlibrary loan procedures are becoming increasingly automated, making them more efficient.

Although the requesting and lending libraries communicate quickly with each other regarding items to be borrowed and loaned, the actual sending of materials back and forth still principally depends on the U.S. Postal Service. But the increasing use of facsimile machines (see C.1.6) in libraries is finally making it possible to speed up the transfer of materials. Interlibrary loan is intended to be reciprocal. Theoretically, a library should loan as much as it borrows; in fact, the load is frequently unbalanced. Various cooperative agreements have been developed to even the load or recompense net lending libraries by net borrowing libraries.

Since many interlibrary loan transactions use photocopies of original materials to satisfy requests, the copyright law (see A.1.5) has an effect on the agreements libraries make when they use interlibrary loan in lieu of purchasing items for their own collections. Library personnel can, however, reproduce library materials to save the content of materials in poor condition so the materials can circulate. Photocopying is also thought to lessen mutilation of library materials; the hope is that users will purchase copies instead of removing pages from items. Preparing circulating reproductions of noncirculating materials also enhances the collections' use.

Circulation encompasses the need for collection security. If an unauthorized removal of an item occurs, that item is no longer available for use—now or in the future. So use must be controlled to preserve the integrity of the library's collections and reduce the cost of replacement. Various methods used to do so include electronic security systems (see C.3.1), reproducing valuable materials to preserve the originals, monitors at all exits to check users' packages and purses for unauthorized removals, and legal penalties for stealing and mutilation. A library must decide whether security should be unobtrusive so as not to discourage lawful use of materials or whether it should be obvious in order to alert users to the need to follow regulations if they want to use the collections and avoid penalties.

B.3.7   **Services**

User services in all kinds of libraries must be based on knowledge about the needs of publics served and about access to materials. Needs of a library's publics are determined by such things as community contacts like advisory or governing boards, news releases, and cooperative planning with community organizations (see A.4.2). Access to materials, involving order and linkage to resources, could be based on only a library's collections, but more likely it will also include access to other institutions' collections (see B.2 and early sections of B.3) and human resources. The extent to which these foundation elements are developed determines the quality of user services at each of the following levels (see B.3.7.1 to B.3.7.4) of service offered in libraries. This hierarchy is based on the paradigm developed by Margaret Monroe and her followers (Margaret E. Monroe, "An Approach to Theoretical Foundations for Reader Services," *Drexel Library Quarterly*, Spring 1983, 21–37). Within each level of the hierarchy, services move from the simple to the complex. As more complicated, increasingly aggressive services are offered, library professionals use their talents to a growing extent. Within the full paradigm, each level evolves from the previous level and is dependent on its predecessor.

All services can be indirect and prepackaged (done ahead of time based on past experience in serving a particular public or in response to requests of specific groups) or direct, personalized, and face-to-face (individualized services for a person or a group as needs are discovered). The following levels of service are valid for all types of libraries, though in some libraries one or more levels may be stressed, depending on the environment, ages, and interests of the publics being served.

B.3.7.1   Information services

In the first service level, libraries provide information; unless librarians and resources are organized to provide an appropriate level of information, it is premature to introduce the following service levels. Information services include whatever is necessary to meet users' needs: for example, organizing open reference collections for self-service; providing quick information face-to-face or by telephone; preparing and distributing subject bibliographies; carrying out in-depth, detailed searches in traditional materials or online databases; gathering files of information for special groups on special topics; preparing abstracts and literature summaries; and establishing special subject information and referral centers. Accuracy, speed, and relevance are important values in information services and are dependent on the context of commitment to service, and order and linkage to resources derived from community contacts and access to materials.

B.3.7.2   Instruction in use of resources

In the second level, instruction is developed to help patrons use resources more efficiently and effectively; instruction focuses on developing users' skills in independent use of the library. This second service level recognizes that the use of professional assistance is costly and scarce and that such assistance should be reserved for more complex problems in information search and materials selection. Instructional services recognize that users need to feel in command of the library and that information-oriented citizens, valuing information as a basis for personal, occupational, and community decision-making, are important to society.

Instruction focuses primarily on increasing library skills through tours and orientation to the library's services, arrangement, and materials; instruction in using the catalog, bibliographies, and reference tools; instruction in using technology such as AV equipment, microform readers, and computer terminals; and instruction in efficiently using all materials, including study skills or critical reading, viewing and listening. Libraries can also attempt instruction in basic literacy skills or the fundamentals of aesthetic appreciation of music or art, though typically these skills are left to specialists in related areas.

The range of instruction provided by a library depends on its mission and the publics it serves. Academic and school libraries support the teaching functions of their parent institutions and often tie much of their instruction to class-related needs. Special libraries may assume they need few instructional services, but could be rewarded with greater user appreciation and involvement if they do increase such services. Public libraries frequently accept adult education as a goal, involving broad support of instructional services to the community. The more effective instruction is in preparing users to deal with what is unique to a particular library, the more widely it is accepted as necessary and legitimate.

B.3.7.3   Guidance to library resources

Guidance constitutes the next level of service and is based on a librarian's knowledge of library resources and his or her interpretation of the material most appropriate to users' needs or interests. The user conveys his or her problem, question, or interest to the librarian, and the librarian guides the user to what may be the most suitable materials. But the user remains in control of the service outcome, and the choice of what materials to actually use lies with him or her. The librarian acts as a facilitator, helping the user clarify needs, explaining possible resources, and helping the user gain access to needed material. Guidance services can include exhibits or programs planned for special group occasions; reading lists on various topics; reading guidance to help in selection of materials for personal use; referral to outside sources that can provide additional help; assistance to an individual planning a personal study program; advice in selecting materials for individuals with personal problems and help in interpreting these materials so the individual derives the greatest benefit; learners' advisory services; and selective dissemination of information based on profiles of users' needs.

The values inherent in guidance services include meeting users' needs and interests with well-selected materials; cooperation between the librarian and user with the final choice of materials made by the user; and encouragement of a user's growth in knowledge or understanding.

B.3.7.4   Stimulating use of materials

Stimulation, the highest level of library service, enables librarians to link their library's resources to the community served in a creative, serendipitous manner. In this level, librarians want to make known a library's wealth of resources. Some activities that stimulate use can be characterized as public relations: mass media announcements, including book lists or reviews in newspapers, on radio, or on television; announcements placed in media channels directed to special groups; library participation in community events; and librarians' presence on local advisory boards and in community groups.

Other stimulating activities create a climate for use: for example, informal conversations with library users and with people in the community about their activities and needs; book displays and film showings; story hours and book talks; concerts and lectures in the library; and reading-readiness programs. The values of stimulating materials use lie in making known the opportunities that are available in libraries and in the professional responsibility to utilize library collections to their greatest depth.

B.3.8 Automation

Automation refers to the automatic operation or control of processes, equipment, or systems. It includes the totality of mechanical and electronic techniques and equipment used to achieve such operations or control. In libraries, it is a tool used to make procedures more efficient and materials more available and to provide services not previously possible using manual methods. (Many specific applications of automation to library procedures have already been mentioned. For fuller explanation of the technology involved see C.5.2.7.)

B.3.9 Preservation and conservation

According to the *ALA Glossary of Library and Information Science* (ALA, 1983), the emerging distinction between conservation and preservation is that conservation refers to the techniques and procedures relating to the treatment of books and other formats to maintain as much as possible their original physical integrity; while preservation includes conservation measures but also encompasses the techniques of partial preservation of the physical object, such as rebinding, as well as the procedures for replacing the original by converting it to other formats, preserving the intellectual content as much as possible.

Most library materials still are constructed primarily of paper, and paper is subject to rapid deterioration when stored in libraries. The causes of such deterioration can be categorized as biological (vermin, mold, fungus), physical (heat, light, moisture), defects (originally acidic paper and ink), and human abuse. Acidic paper, whether resulting from the paper-making process or caused by increasing pollution in the atmosphere, interacting with temperature (high temperatures speed up chemical reactions caused by acidity, which ultimately speeds up deterioration) appears to be the major cause of paper destruction.

Efforts to reduce any of these causes affect interdependent aspects of library processes. If libraries attempt to acquire only materials containing alkaline-buffered paper, the selection of library materials may be severely hampered because many paper manufacturers do not regard libraries as major consumers of their products. Lowering libraries' temperature can hinder physical access to materials, as can dimming the lights or putting them on timers. Systematic inspection for fungal and rodent damage may require more staff time than can be provided. User-operated photocopying machines may reduce mutilation of materials, and certainly do provide a service demanded by the public, but their misuse also damages bindings and stresses content.

Formats that are not paper-based also require care to ensure their continual availability. The film base used for microformats must be processed correctly to avoid deterioration of the image, and the durability of some types of film is uncertain. Machine-readable data files are subject to outside, often unpredictable magnetic disruption, and the permanence of these files is also unclear at present. Regular use can deteriorate the content of any format; such wear is to be expected and is inherent in offering library materials for use, but preservation methods attempt to lengthen the format's expected period of use beyond what it would be if no efforts were made.

Preservation efforts in libraries can involve a multitude of activities: developing an understanding of paper deterioration; encouraging the development and use of alkaline wood-pulp paper; preparing and safely storing microfilm masters; controlling the storage environment; instituting archivally sound repair techniques; carefully selecting and monitoring commercial binders; promptly binding and repairing deteriorating materials; constructing protective boxes and wrappers; identifying and managing brittle books; and educating staff and users. Disaster recovery and prevention plans are also part of any thorough preservation program. Rare book conservation has been an important part of many libraries' operations for some time, but it is increasingly being recognized and accepted that all library materials can be in danger of premature destruction, and preservation measures need to be extended to all materials a library plans to keep past the point of immediate need.

Preservation activities should be incorporated in other library processes and become a permanent part of their activities. Collection management plans (see B.3.1) need to incorporate preservation schemes; acquisitions activities (see B.3.2) need to consider the durability of projected purchases in terms of assumed use; and processing services (see B.3.3) need to avoid actions that may start the deterioration cycle. The storage of library materials (see B.3.5) is a major influence on materials' length of survival; and whether materials are allowed to circulate or not, the type of security imposed also affects the longevity of materials (see B.3.6).

The need to preserve library materials can conflict with the needs of users to access collections, but preservation activities are also designed to ensure that users can continue to access these collections for a longer time. The catastrophe that could occur if library collections continue their deterioration is fairly well understood now, and there is growing awareness by both librarians and users that something must be done to avert it.

Larry N. Osborne

C. TECHNOLOGY

C.1 Office

While much of the glamour of technology is in the high-tech areas of computers or communications, technological advances in simple office equipment may have had a greater overall impact on the provision of information. One need only consider the revolution resulting from the elimination of hand-written catalog cards to appreciate what effect an improvement in office equipment can have on library operations.

C.1.1 Typewriters

Typewriters are fundamental to library operations, as they are to most organizations. Despite the promise of word processing, much work is still hammered out on typewriters and will probably continue to be for some time.

There are three main kinds of typewriters: manual, electric, and electronic. The venerable manual, or mechanical, typewriter may be considered the device that began the office automation revolution. Even fully automated offices often keep one or two mechanical typewriters in case their electric counterparts break or the office loses power. Some offices continue to use them exclusively, finding that they are more reliable and cheaper to repair.

With a mechanical typewriter, the typist's finger depresses a key that, through a chain of ratchets and levers, causes a typebar to move in an arc to bring the type in contact with an ink-coated fabric ribbon, which in turn is pressed with force against the document, or sheet of paper, producing the printed character. As each character is typed, the carriage that holds the document is moved one space to the left, positioning the paper for the next stroke. At the end of a line, the typist pushes a lever that simultaneously moves the paper to the next line and returns the carriage to the far right.

The electric typewriter was an improvement on the manual models, since impression could be made constant and the finger pressure necessary to create a letter could be reduced. The earliest models were simply first power-assisted manuals, but a true advance was made when IBM brought out its Selectric in the 1960s. This typewriter sported, in addition to a keyboard that has never been improved upon, a total lack of typebars and of the traditional paper carriage. Typebars were replaced by a ball-shaped element that was pivoted by thin metal bands, rotating it until the proper letter was selected, and the carriage was replaced by maintaining the paper in a constant position while the typing element moved across it. These two improvements allowed the virtual elimination of misaligned letters and an increase in typing speed. Also, these improvements, combined with a carbon-coated mylar ribbon instead of an ink-coated fabric one, allowed near-printed quality. While IBM held the patent for the Selectric mechanism, several other companies developed similar machines, some with daisy wheel elements that carried type characters on strips arranged in a star pattern.

Excellent as it was, the IBM Selectric did have some disadvantages, notably a relatively high price and an exceptionally complex mechanism. As digital technology advanced, it became obvious that a marriage of the dot-matrix printer (see C.5.2.1.1.2.1.2) and the typewriter would result in significant savings in both money and complexity. Several manufacturers introduced such electronic machines, often with microprocessors and rudimentary data storage facilities. Such refinements allow typists to correct copy and then retype the document and, in some cases, to temporarily store a document for later recall. Some electronic typewriters can store an entire line in memory until the line is finished, then type it all at once. This allows the typist to correct a line before it is printed.

IBM has taken a slightly different approach and has combined the Selectric chassis with the data storage and correction features of the electronic typewriter to produce a formed-character rather than a dot matrix electronic typewriter. Some of these models can be considered low-end microcomputers.

C.1.2   **Word processors**

Word processors use computer technology (see C.5) to manipulate textual material. As such, they contain the three basic elements of any computer system: an input device (normally a CRT (cathode ray tube) terminal and keyboard), a CPU (central processing unit), and an output device (commonly a printer of some sort). All word processing units also include some form of storage, either floppy disks or a harddisk unit. Sometimes word processors are purchased as stand-alone units; that is, specialized computers that are dedicated entirely to word processing. It may make more economic sense, however, to purchase a general purpose computer and then purchase the necessary word processing software. In either case, word processors perform certain necessary functions.

One function is receiving and manipulating text. Every word processor must be able to create text files, allow new text to be inserted at specified places in the file, delete unwanted material, and replace unwanted material with new material. These are sometimes referred to as the add, delete, and change functions of word processors and are absolutely essential. Other common text-manipulation attributes of word processing systems include the ability to move blocks of text from one place to another (cut and paste), to copy blocks of text within the manuscript, and to allow insertion of one document within another.

The second fundamental task of a word processor is the production of an attractive document. This function, commonly referred to as formatting, encompasses page length, margins, indentions, underlining, boldfacing, and so on, which result in a manuscript with a layout that meets reader expectations. In addition to the basic format functions, some word processors can easily modify the output from pica (10 characters per inch, also known as 10 pitch), to elite (12 characters per inch, or 12 pitch), or to proportionally spaced (which produces a near-typeset appearance by allowing each letter to take up an amount of space equivalent to its width rather than printing a fixed number of characters per inch).

In addition to these common characteristics of word processors, vendors normally add extras to make their products more attractive and therefore more likely to be purchased. While some of these are mere whistles and bells, some are true enhancements. Of these, some of the most useful or common include on-screen formatting (which allows a document to be viewed in its final form before printing begins), spelling checkers (usually called dictionaries), and windows (the ability to view two files or two parts of the same file at once). Some manufacturers also add thesauri, grammar checkers, automatic footnoting, and indexing and table of contents production.

Less common, and relatively expensive, word processing functions include the ability to store and manipulate graphics material (both pictures and graphs) and to accept input in the form of printed material. This last function, a refinement of OCR (optical character recognition) technology, is of special interest to information scientists because it permits the inputting of text for later manipulation, retrieval, or transmittal without the time and effort of hand typing it.

Word processors may be purchased as a complete turnkey system (computer and program) or as components. General purpose microcomputers are often used with suitable software (for example, Word Perfect or Microsoft Word) for word processing.

C.1.3   **Desktop publishing**

In the past, documents having complex formats (such as newsletters), requiring a fine appearance (such as brochures or annual reports), or requiring print in varying sizes or styles were created by providing typescript marked with special instructions (specifications) to printers for typesetting. Illustrations, graphs, photographs, and other graphics elements were added after the typeset copy was created.

This process, while allowing publishers to inspect the finished product and creating a quality document, was expensive and often slow. Revisions made after the type was set often required that the entire process be done again at additional cost and more delay, yet until the finished product was delivered, only the most experienced could foresee the end result. This lack of immediate feedback, coupled with time pressure, often necessitated accepting marginal products.

Desktop publishing was created to help overcome these difficulties. It uses word processing techniques coupled with high-quality printers (see C.5.2.1.1.2.3), graphics input devices (see C.5.2.1.1), and special page-oriented software (see C.5.2.6) to produce near-typeset-quality pages.

In a typical desktop publishing environment, text is entered by a word processing program directly into the personal computer (see C.5.2.4.3), which will be used for the entire desktop publishing process. This basic document is modified by changing the type style, or font, the type size, and the document's layout. Graphics elements are then added to make up a complete page, which is then sent to a high-quality printer (see figure 1). The document's creator has control of the entire process and is able to modify it immediately at any stage because the apparatus is, literally, on his or her desk.

The document's creator usually makes these modifications while observing the page's appearance on a monitor, but it is possible (while simultaneously reducing efficiency and immediacy of feedback) to perform such tasks by embedding commands in the text file, which are then interpreted by the page description program when the document is printed.

The Apple Macintosh is the machine most closely identified with desktop publishing, but IBM and other machines can also be used with the addition of supplementary hardware and appropriate software. The documents produced by desktop publishing will not be as good as those produced by traditional typesetting techniques, but unless printed on glossy paper, the difference is hardly noticeable. If true typeset quality is needed, some typesetting facilities can accept the computer file produced by a word processor and use it to create the necessary product.

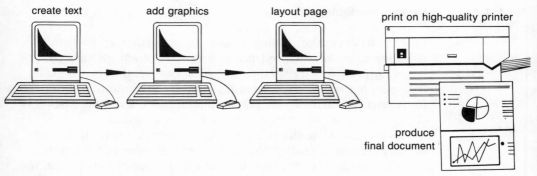

create text   add graphics   layout page   print on high-quality printer

produce
final document

Fig. 1. Steps in desktop publishing

C.1.4   Electronic mail

Electronic mail (EM) offers a way to pass memos, messages, letters, or other information from one individual to another using electronic means. It thus reproduces the current hard-copy mail system in an electronic form but offers the possibility of linking directly to other electronic systems such as personal computers or word processors. Electronic message systems have been standard on large computer systems for many years, and networks of single-manufacturer computer users have maintained messaging systems, but the commercial availability of such systems has come about only recently.

In its simplest form, electronic mail consists of the ability to leave messages for other users of a computer system. The message receiver, upon logging on, or accessing, the computer, is informed of the waiting message and has the option to read and reply to it. In multilocation situations, such as in branches of a single company, messages may be passed by telephone from computer to computer, and in situations where, for example, telephone lines are leased but not utilized fully, such communications may be extremely cost effective.

Electronic mail, as a form of communications, has the major benefit of speed but may also be more secure and facilitate filing. Once these benefits became known, and spurred by the breakup of the AT&T monopoly, several commercial vendors began to offer electronic mail services. These vendors include traditional agencies like Western Union, Federal Express, and the U.S. Post Office; new firms devoted to electronic messaging such as MCI; commercial computer time sharing systems such as CompuServe and The Source; and order and accounting departments of various commercial firms, including banks and large book vendors.

Currently, there are many electronic mail options available to libraries; they range from systems suitable for a single department or small library to national utilities allowing messages to be exchanged transcontinentally. (For example, when a local area network (see C.5.2.5.4) is installed, electronic mail is usually included with the software package.) Whether the communications are local or distant, however, the transactions themselves are similar. In a typical system, the first step is to prepare a document, often by using a word processor. This document may be a letter, a report, a book order, an authorization to transfer funds, or any other information that must be sent to another location. The second step is to establish electronic communications. These communications can be established directly between the sender and receiver, that is, one word processor may communicate directly with another word processor, or indirectly through one or more intermediate locations, or nodes. (For example, a personal computer in the sender's library may connect to another personal computer in a different library through that library's main computer, to a computer in an EM vendor's home office, to the main computer in a book vendor's headquarters, to a smaller computer in the order department, to a personal computer on the receiver's desk.) Obviously, if the sender and receiver nodes are directly connected, the message may be passed immediately; but if the receiver and sender are both communicating with some intermediate location, the message may need to be stored at that location until the receiver contacts it to receive, or download, the communication. (See figure 2.)

If the receiver sends a reply, these steps are repeated from the other end. The communications links in the above scenario may be part of the national telephone network, part of a local area network (see C.5.2.5.4) within a single organization, or sent through individual cables connecting the nodes. Normally, the electronic mail user is unaware of the actual transmission path his or her message follows. Unfortunately, this transparency does not extend to the actual commands required to send the message. While providers of EM services are attempting to simplify the process, sending a message does require a user to know the commands necessary to access the other nodes and to tell the processors at the nodes what to do with the message. Of course, both parties must be authorized to use the service.

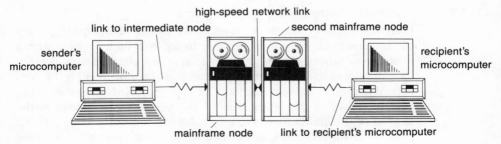

Fig. 2. Components of electronic mail

In addition to these basic uses, electronic mail also has the potential for voice mail (storage and forwarding of spoken or electronically synthesized messages), teleconferencing (a technique whereby many individuals can pass messages readable to all between each other—in effect an electronic conference), as well as linking to telefacsimile and other more traditional services.

While the above explanation may sound complicated, the process quickly becomes second nature; and as vendors increase the transparency of their systems (that is, make the mechanics of communications less obvious to users), the time spent learning a system's peculiarities is becoming shorter. In fact, electronic mail is rapidly integrating with other office automation functions such as word processing and data storage and retrieval. This leads to the current situation where it is quite possible for a document to be prepared in electronic form via word processing, be transmitted via electronic mail, be read and replied to, with both the original and reply filed, without ever appearing in hard copy.

C.1.5   Copying machines

Copying machines have largely replaced carbon paper and have gone far toward replacing paper and pencil for note taking. A writer copies the relevant portions of references, then writes a new document. The document is sent off, but not before it is copied.

Copiers may be divided into three groups: those using heat to transfer an image, those using static electricity, and those using light.

C.1.5.1   Heat transfer copiers

Heat transfer machines use a paper containing chemicals that discolor at a specific temperature.. When an original document (sometimes via an intermediate step) is placed in contact with the paper and then exposed to heat, the darker characters absorb more heat than the lighter paper; therefore, the coated paper discolors to match the characters on the original.

The heat transfer process is simple and inexpensive, but the quality of the copy is not good and the process is slow.

C.1.5.2   Electrical (electrostatic) transfer copiers

Electrical transfer machines, commonly called xerographic or dry copiers, are the copiers most popular today. A cylinder coated with a selenium or other light-sensitive material is first charged with electricity and then exposed to a projected image of the document to be copied. Where the amount of light in the projected image is high, corresponding to the white area of the original, the charge is destroyed. The cylinder rotates to pass a dry ink substance (toner) with a negative charge. This substance is naturally attracted to the remaining charge on the cylinder, which corresponds to the darker part of the

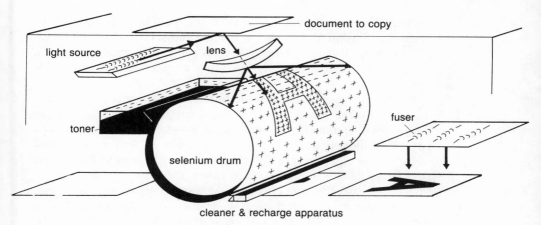

light source · lens · document to copy · toner · selenium drum · fuser · cleaner & recharge apparatus

Fig. 3. Electrical transfer machine

projected image: the characters on the original. While the toner and the image have opposite charges, not all the negative charge of the toner is canceled. A sheet of paper that has been positively charged is passed across the cylinder and attracts the toner. The paper and toner are then exposed to heat, which fuses the toner to the paper, producing a quality copy. (See figure 3.)

An alternative to the cylinder technique is to use a coated sheet of paper that is itself photoconductive. In these machines, a few of which use liquid toner, the image is generally made permanent by pressure rather than heat. Because they require special paper, such machines are not as versatile as plain-paper copiers.

C.1.5.3 Light transfer (photochemical) copiers

Copiers that use light to transfer an image produce the familiar blue-print. A variant of the Diazo process, which used specific nitrogeneous chemicals, the light transfer technique requires special paper. A very strong light is shined directly through the original document, exposing the copy beneath. Obviously, more light goes through the paper where it is blank. This light modifies the chemicals in the paper's coating. The paper is then exposed to another chemical that, when combined with the original coating, forms a dark substance. The area exposed to light, since its coating was chemically modified, remains white. A variant of this process uses ammonia vapor to activate the chemicals.

While not a common process, the Diazo technique is often used to reproduce microfilms and to make copies of architectural and engineering documents.

C.1.6 Facsimile

Facsimile equipment is similar to the electrical transfer copiers discussed above in that it uses light to convert an original document to an electrical form. In facsimile, this takes the form of lines made up of pixels (the portion of the image converted at one time). Standard resolutions are 67, 96, and 200 lpi (scan lines per inch). Generally, text can be scanned at the lower resolution, while graphics require the higher resolution.

The output from older facsimile equipment was generally analog in nature, with strength of the signal being proportional to tone of the image. Such equipment was slow, requiring several minutes to scan a page, but allowed transmission of gray tones as well as black and white. Newer equipment is digital and thus two-state: black or white. Digital facsimile is, however, much faster than analog techniques.

In either case, the signal is usually sent over telephone lines to a receiving apparatus, which changes the strength of a light source in step with the signal. This light is used, as in the electrical transfer copiers, to create an image on paper.

While compatibility of machines from different vendors was a problem in the past, recent attempts at standardization appear to be succeeding. Other problems that led libraries and information services to virtually abandon facsimile techniques after a brief spurt of interest in the 1960s include the cost and complexity of equipment, and hence its fragility, and the often poor quality of reproduction. More recently, lower cost, improved dependability, decreased long-distance telephone charges, and the simplicity of digital transmission techniques, coupled with the availability of special circuit boards that allow microcomputers to function as facsimile machines, have resulted in another wave of interest in facsimile apparatus. For organizations that cannot justify the expense of maintaining their own machines, commercial networks with telefacsimile capabilities are available.

C.2   Communications

Communications is important not only as it relates to receiving queries and transmitting responses, but also during intermediate stages of LIS (library and information science) operations. Note that this section deals with the technology of communications, not with its psychological or sociological aspects.

C.2.1   Wired

Wired communications include all communications forms where messages are transmitted through transfer of electrons; however, this type of communications is often considered synonymous with telephone service. While the most common wired communications form is a twisted pair (a two-conductor cable), multiconductor circuits are common, and at distances greater than about a mile, the solid wire becomes conceptual because amplifiers are necessary to boost signal

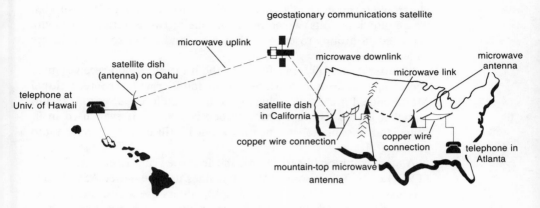

Fig. 4. Example of microwave antenna communication

strength. For practical purposes, communications circuits that termi-nate in physical wires can be considered as wired even if some other form of transmission (for example, a microwave) takes place during an intervening stage. (See figure 4.)

C.2.1.1   Voice

Voice grade lines, the type generally used in business or domestic tele-phone service, are capable of transmitting signals in the range of 300 to 3,000 Hz (Hertz, or cycles per second). This is only a portion of the nominal 20 to 20,000 Hz range perceived by human ears and causes the "telephone sound" people associate with such communications. Actu-ally, this range limitation is largely a result of the repeating amplifiers used by the telephone industry and not the wire or other apparatus. In situations where better fidelity is important, lines may be equalized in order to provide a wider and more flat frequency response.

Equipment used for voice communications over telephone wires ranges from the venerable basic-black Western Electric telephone to sophisticated local switching systems with call forwarding, conferenc-ing, and limited-access features.

With the breakup of AT&T, shopping for telephone service has be-come more complex. Access to the network, internal wiring, telephone receivers, and long-distance services may all be purchased, and in some cases *must* be purchased, from different vendors.

C.2.1.2   Data

Voice or other sound communications begin as compression, or sound, waves moving through the atmosphere that must be changed into electromagnetic waves for transmission over telephone lines. Data communications imply that the data to be transmitted are already in electronic form; normally, this electronic form is binary digits, or bits. These individual bits, which represent one of two electrical states, are arranged in groups to encode characters and when so arranged are called bytes.

In order to usefully transfer data, the transmitter and receiver must agree on the code used. Most people are familiar with the international Morse code, for example, which uses short and long pulses to transmit alphabet letters. However, Morse code is seldom, if ever, used in library and information science work but is still used by several radio services.

A more common library code is the Teletypewriter Exchange Service (TWX) code. While some TWX machines use the newer ASCII code (discussed in the following paragraph), others use a five-bit, or five-level, code in which each letter or other character is represented by a unique sequence of five binary digits. TELEX, telegraph, and news service codes are similar, although not identical. Each of these services uses its own code and its own machines, and they are not interchangeable. For these services, a machine very like an electric typewriter converts the motion of depressing a key into the proper code while also producing the appropriate printed character. The code is then transmitted to its destination, usually over standard telephone lines commonly referred to as switched telephone lines. There the signal is converted into its proper characters and printed on paper.

Computers, rather than use five-level codes, generally exchange data through a standardized seven-bit code called the American Standard Code for Information Interchange (ASCII), although some computers—notably large IBM machines—use their own codes under certain circumstances. While ASCII is nominally a seven-level code (that is, each character is represented by seven bits), an error-checking bit called a parity bit is commonly also transmitted. When this is done, it is proper to refer to ASCII as an eight-level code. There are also extended ASCII codes that use the eighth bit to allow additional characters (for example, those characters used by languages other than English or graphics characters).

In order to transmit computer-produced data over telephone lines, two tasks must be accomplished. First, the character must be converted from the computer's internal storage convention into ASCII code. This is generally done by the computer. The second task is to convert the ASCII character in its two-state electrical form into a form that can easily be sent over switched telephone lines.

Simplistically, at one end of the circuit, a special tone is produced and then modified, or modulated, by tones of different frequencies corresponding to the two states of the bits making up the character. At the other end, the tones are demodulated, or converted back to electronic states, for acceptance by the computer. The device that modu-

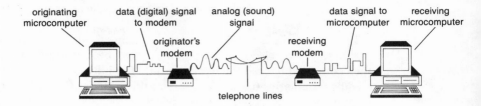

Fig. 5. Data communication

lates and demodulates the signal is called a modem (a contraction of modulator/demodulator) or occasionally a dataset. (See figure 5.)

While this basic form of modem operation usually is used only at speeds of fewer than 120 characters per second (1,200 baud), analogous techniques allow much higher speed transfer with speeds of 2,400, 4,800 and even 9,600 BPS (bits per second) becoming available. The rough equivalency of 10 baud equaling 1 character per second holds true at lower speeds but breaks down at higher ones.

C.2.1.3   Combination

Most telephone services now operating are essentially analog in nature, that is, they use signals that vary in proportion to the sounds being sent over them and therefore require conversion by modem when digital signals are to be communicated. This communications form is largely a historical accident, and if all communications paths were designed for digital communications, both the speed and quantity of information transfer could be increased. Telefacsimile, television, digital, and voice signals could be sent over such a system, eliminating much duplication of effort.

While no large-scale integrated service digital network (ISDN), as such services are called, now exists, there is no doubt that such networks will soon be developed. Of course, the equipment now producing analog signals, such as ordinary telephones, would need to be converted, but it appears the benefits will outweigh the disadvantages, at least for large-volume users.

C.2.2   **Optical**

Using light rather than wire to transmit signals is not a new idea; Alexander Graham Bell produced such a device. But after many years of being overshadowed by its metal cousin, light transmission is exciting interest. Part of this increasing interest is because fiber optics can carry more messages at a higher transmission rate than wire, partly due to the decreased signal loss and interference associated with light transmission, and partly because it is relatively immune to nuclear attack. Fiber optics is also more difficult to tap, although whether this is an advantage or disadvantage depends on its application and the user's point of view.

Light generally is not the primary data senders wish to transmit. Instead, sound or electrical signals must first be converted into light, then converted back at the receiving end. The initial conversion is handled by modulating a laser or light-emitting diode (LED), while any of several photosensitive solid-state devices can be used to convert the signal back at the end of its path. Devices that combine both functions in a single package are called transceivers.

Over short distances, like their wired counterparts, fiber optic transmissions need no amplification; on longer runs, light transmissions need fewer repeaters, or amplifiers, than wire transmissions because of the low signal losses associated with properly installed optical cable. Telephone longlines and underseas cables have already been installed using optical technology, and local communications, although still limited by input and output costs, are increasingly switching to lightguides.

There is no single type of optical fiber for all applications. Available fibers are graded according to construction, and therefore refraction characteristics, which in turn cause differences in propagation parameters. All three main types of optical fibers (described below) are composed of an internal core that actually transmits the light, and a form of cladding that surrounds the core. Additional layers are often added for physical protection and support.

C.2.2.1   Step index fibers

Step index fibers have an abrupt transition between core and cladding refraction indexes. They are relatively inexpensive and easy to splice and interface but suffer more signal loss than the other types. They are typically used in local communications.

C.2.2.2   Graded index fibers

Graded index fibers have a refraction index that changes steadily from the center of the core to a level equal to the cladding. They suffer less signal loss but are harder to splice and interface. They are generally used in medium-distance telephone communications.

C.2.2.3   Single-mode fibers

Single-mode fibers have an abrupt change in refraction and are characterized by a much smaller core than the others. Light in a single-mode fiber travels straight down the middle of its core rather than bouncing off the cladding as in the other two types. This results in much less signal loss and distortion, allowing more signals to travel over greater distances, but they are exceptionally difficult to splice and interface. They are therefore employed only in longline service.

94

C.2.3   **Freespace**

Freespace communications, often simply called radio, employ electromagnetic waves propagated in the open rather than the flow of electrons through a wire or light through a lightguide. Many communications thought of as wired (for example, switched telephone circuits) actually are often transmitted via microwave, or high-frequency, radio.

Radio can be an attractive alternative to other communications media, especially when access to telephones is awkward or nonexistent, such as in vehicles. It is convenient to divide radio communications into local communications (which involve direct reception of a transmitted signal and which are relatively inexpensive ways of covering areas the size of a city or perhaps a county) and remote communications (which, by using apparatus that receive, amplify, and retransmit the signal, are capable of covering much larger areas).

C.2.3.1   Local

Local communications via radio fall into two primary categories: communications using frequencies assigned specifically to public service organizations, and communications using frequencies available to private citizens for personal communications.

C.2.3.1.1   Utility band

Using frequencies assigned to public services has the advantage of being relatively secure (bearing in mind that no radio communications truly can be considered secure) and generally free from interference, both natural and artificial. The utility band provides dependable communications over the areas library and information science (LIS) organizations are likely to cover, such as counties. The equipment, however, is fairly expensive, and the licensing requirements, while not complex or technical, do require care.

C.2.3.1.2   Citizen's band

The common citizen's band (CB) radio also may be used for local communications. Such apparatus is much less expensive than the typical utility band equipment and is available from more sources. It is also easier to obtain licenses for such equipment. Countering these advantages are potential disadvantages. Because the citizen's band is open to the public, communications frequencies are sometimes crowded and are subject to interference (sometimes malicious interference) by other operators. The citizen's bands' total lack of security may be either a disadvantage or free advertising, depending on the mission of the communicator.

C.2.3.2   Remote

Radio communications of distances greater than those associated with the equipment discussed above are also possible and practical.

C.2.3.2.1   Ground-to-ground

Direct communications over long distances by individuals or LIS institutions are seldom accomplished by radio today. Nonetheless, private microwave facilities should not be ruled out, especially for data communications, since appreciable savings over private wired systems may be possible. When such ground-to-ground communications are used, the preferred method is via line-of-sight transmission using very high frequency signals, or microwaves, with repeaters strategically spaced to receive, amplify, and retransmit the message as needed.

C.2.3.2.2   Via satellite

While only a few years ago satellite communications by small organizations were only a science fiction scenario, they are well established, if not common, today. Satellite communications are especially attractive when long distances are combined with a need for certainty of access, that is, when private or leased telephone lines would be the alternative. Obviously, they are almost necessary when organizations must hold frequent, lengthy communications with, for example, the Pacific Islands. While few LIS institutions can purchase and deploy their own satellites, commercial communications companies like COMSAT will lease channels or time.

C.2.4   Cellular telephone

An interesting and potentially useful melding of communications technologies is the cellular telephone (sometimes called cellular radio) services that are beginning to become common in large population centers. The service commonly called mobile telephone normally uses a single high-power transmitter to reach a local area often specified arbitrarily as fifty miles. Each conversation occupies the transmitter, and in order to add additional circuits, additional transmission frequencies are required. This is expensive.

Cellular telephone services, on the other hand, use many low-powered transmitters. Each transmission site contains several transmitters that communicate with remote transceivers (transmitter/receiver units). Each service area is divided into many cells, each of which can handle several simultaneous conversations; therefore, the number of telephones that can be active over the entire service area is much larger than in a traditional mobile telephone network. Indeed, cellular systems are said to be able to handle almost one hundred times the number of simultaneous conversations that conventional systems can handle. (See figure 6.)

The cost of this increased service is increased complexity. A sophisticated computer at each cell transmission site keeps track of where the remote unit is and, at the appropriate time, hands that unit over to an adjacent cell. To accomplish this function, each transceiver is a double

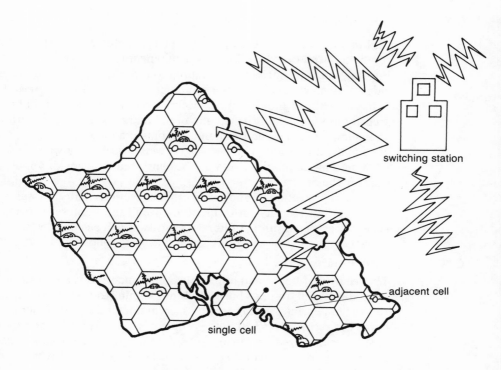

switching station

adjacent cell

single cell

Fig. 6. Cellular phone network. The two cells would have separate switching stations.

system capable of sending and receiving signals over two frequencies at the same time: one for voice and one for data, as well as a microprocessor. The cell sites, in turn, are controlled by a single switching office that links the radio signals to the ordinary telephone service.

C.2.5   **Pneumatic**

Pneumatic communications are included here largely in the interest of historical completeness, since such schemes were not uncommon earlier in the century and some may still be in use. Pneumatic transmission generally was used only within a single building. It consisted of airtight tubing running from department to department. Air was constantly evacuated from one end of this system, causing atmospheric pressure that created a wind capable of moving carefully sized hollow cylinders containing written messages.

Such systems, while generally secure and dependable, were no competition for electric data transmission systems or internal telephone systems.

C.3   Security

"Library security" is a broad term. It includes protection of personnel (both staff and users), collections, equipment, physical facilities, and information from such harm as mutilation, theft, physical attack, accidental damage, and what the insurance industry calls acts of god.

In line with the broad scope of security problems, successful library security programs must be equally broad and must involve integrated strategies: personnel, policies, and equipment all have their place and are equally important. This section, however, deals only with the last of these. This emphasis should not be construed as a lack of appreciation for the others.

Because protection of books and other collections materials was one of the earliest security problems recognized, and because it forms a generally accepted subset of library security, it will be considered first, with the more recent and more general aspects following.

C.3.1   Book security

The security of books and other collections materials is a necessary, if often distasteful, responsibility of library administration. Loss rates of five to ten percent per year are not uncommon, and much higher rates have been recorded. Whether the problem is called theft or the euphemistic unauthorized borrowing, a book that is removed from a collection without proper recording may cause legitimate user requests to go unmet.

There are many nontechnological approaches to materials theft prevention, including guards, physical checks of patrons' packages, minimizing egress (locking unneeded doors), closing stacks, and even the mundane bookstamp. However, almost all successful techniques suffer to some degree from obtrusiveness, that is, they cause problems for honest as well as dishonest patrons.

Electronic systems largely overcome this disadvantage. Except for requiring patrons to leave the library through narrowly defined exits, an honest or unforgetful patron is usually unaware that he or she is being checked. It is no wonder that these systems were greeted with enthusiasm when they first appeared in the 1960s.

C.3.1.1   Principles of operation

There are two main modes of book theft detection operation: passive and active. Although most library systems are active, some are a hybrid or variation of passive and active; both modes have been used and therefore both are covered here.

C.3.1.1.1   Passive systems

In passive systems, some form of magnetized material is placed in the book or other item. When the item is brought within the range of a detector, an alarm is set off. Such a system generates no electromagnetic energy and hence does not cause interference and is not even a potential health hazard. Unfortunately, such purely passive systems generally suffer from false alarms and lack of sensitivity and therefore are seldom found today.

C.3.1.1.2   Active systems

Active systems use some form of a reradiation or reflection principle. A special strip, laminate, or panel is placed in the item to be secured. When exposed to an electromagnetic field, the signal is reflected or reradiated in such a way that the presence of the special device is detected and an alarm is set off.

While no health hazards have been proven, such systems do emit electromagnetic radiation. Some produce a strong enough signal that they do not meet European health standards. Others might conceivably cause interference with pacemakers, degrade magnetic computer media, or interfere with electronic communications.

C.3.1.2   Single-state systems

The simplest book security system is the single-state version. In this case, the system is always armed: any attempt to pass the sensing elements with a protected item will set off the alarm. Under this system, protected items must be passed around the sensing area to be picked up on the other side by the patron. This inconvenience, always a reminder that security measures are being taken, is the largest disadvantage of one-state systems. On the other hand, since the activating element need not change state, the system can make use of more robust activating elements. In other words, there is less chance that a patron can shield or deactivate the operating device.

C.3.1.3   Two-state systems

Two-state systems use elements that can be made to either set off the alarm or not, depending on the way they are manipulated. In a typical two-state system, a fluctuating magnetic field is used to change the physical state of the activating elements. For example, elements can be magnetized, or small dipole elements can be aligned to cause the activating elements to reflect radio waves coherently.

Once in this sensitized state, the activating elements are easily sensed by the detection devices that commonly parallel the client's exit path. If a patron attempts to carry library material through this path without first desensitizing the material, an alarm will be triggered. Such desensitization must be one step in the book charging process and generally is done by exposing the sensitized elements to an alternating current electromagnet, which produces a magnetic field, much as a recording tape is erased. Of course, resensitizing the material must also be a part of the check-in process. (See figure 7.)

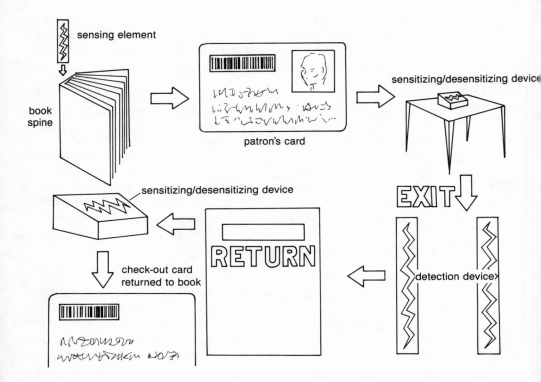

book spine

sensing element

patron's card

sensitizing/desensitizing device

sensitizing/desensitizing device

EXIT

RETURN

detection device

check-out card returned to book

Fig. 7. Book theft protection. The sensing element, hidden in the book spine, is desensitized when the book is checked out. Thus no alarm sounds when the patron goes through the detection device. When the book is returned, it is sensitized and checked in.

C.3.1.4   Preparing books

For either form of theft detection, books to be protected must be processed to include the activating device. These devices vary from system to system but generally take the form of thin strips, bookplates, labels, or tags. Since these devices are not a minor investment in the quantities necessary to completely protect a medium or large library, especially when coupled with the cost of labor required to apply them, many libraries compromise by protecting all new books and a portion of older materials. Since many of the elements are difficult for patrons to detect, an occasional alarm will give the impression that all books are marked.

It should also be noted that permanently sensitized elements are available for most book security systems. Such labels would be applied to reference and reserve materials in order to prevent their accidental circulation.

C.3.2   **Plant security**

Preventing people from stealing library materials using book theft detection systems or more traditional means is analogous to shoplifting
prevention in commercial establishments. While such security is necessary, it is not sufficient. Libraries must also guard against unauthorized intrusion, mutilation of library materials, physical violence, and
natural disasters. Such concerns are discussed below.

C.3.2.1   Surveillance

One commonly used technique for preventing crime is to take away the
privacy necessary for its commission. However, such surveillance also
infringes on the privacy of people not intent on committing crimes,
and this concern must be balanced with that of detecting and preventing crime. Because of the reluctance of clients and staff to be under
constant scrutiny, such an approach is normally used only in non-
private areas such as halls and parking lots and in high-crime areas.

The most common form of surveillance is to have a guard or library
staff member make the rounds periodically. However, when personnel
is insufficient for such surveillance, closed circuit television (CCTV) is
commonly used. Under this scheme, a television camera is mounted to
prevent its being vandalized but so it still can command a view of the
surveillance area. Refinements to this basic arrangement include wide-
angle or zoom lenses, panning (swiveling) camera mounts, and video
recorders to make a record of observations.

A series of such cameras can be wired to a single location where
staff can observe the surveillance areas either on a set of monitors or,
using a sequential switching mechanism, on a single monitor. When
such a switching arrangement is used, an override is provided so that,
when necessary, a single camera can be selected for protracted observation.

The crime prevention value of CCTV is dependent on potential
criminals knowing of its presence. Therefore, for maximum effectiveness, a system should be obvious. There is no value in hiding cameras
or monitors. Prominent signs pointing out the use of television surveillance should be posted. Of course, this means that special effort
should be made to vandal-proof the installation. On the other hand,
the *belief* that a television system has been installed is often a sufficient
deterrent. Therefore, some protection can be gained by installing
dummy cameras in likely locations.

Both CCTV monitors and cameras need not be of broadcast quality
but must accommodate widely varying levels of light. If existing light
does not provide acceptable picture quality, additional light must be
provided. If it cannot be provided, image intensifiers, which concentrate light and allow viewing under low light situations, or infrared
camera elements can be used at greater expense.

Finally, in situations where common coaxial cable cannot conveniently be used, either free-space broadcasting using slow-scan techniques or laser transmissions can be used to transmit pictures from cameras to monitors.

C.3.2.2   Intruder detection

Intruders are people who are where they are not supposed to be or are in public areas when they should not be there. As such, some intruders can be discovered by using the surveillance equipment discussed above, but many libraries cannot afford a round-the-clock guard and must depend on security technology to make up the deficiency.

Intruder detection systems may be divided into two types: passive and active.

C.3.2.2.1   Passive systems

Passive intruder detection systems do not radiate any sonic or electromagnetic waves. Examples of such devices are magnetic switches, breakable foil and wire conductors, pressure-sensitive devices, light-change detectors, capacitance-change detectors, and sound detectors.

C.3.2.2.1.1   Magnetic switches

When the magnet of a magnetic switch is moved, perhaps by a door or window being opened, it causes the switch to open or close, activating an alarm signal.

C.3.2.2.1.2   Breakable foil and wire

In this simple system, a wire or strip of flat foil that serves the same purpose is attached across possible points of entrance, such as windows. If the foil or wire is broken during entrance, the interruption of electrical current causes an alarm to sound.

C.3.2.2.1.3   Pressure-sensitive devices

Pressure-sensitive devices, often in the form of mats, are placed beneath windows, in front of doors, and so on. When an intruder steps on this device, the pressure causes the circuit to close, which sounds an alarm. This is the same technique some supermarkets use to open doors automatically for customers.

C.3.2.2.1.4   Light-change devices

When a photoelectric detector similar to the detectors used in photographic light meters is used in a circuit, a change in light level will sound an alarm, just as changing light moves a needle in a light meter. The only likely source of a change in light level in a library after hours would be the activities of intruders. Of course, for light-change devices and other detectors that monitor change, provision must be made for slow changes due to normal environmental variations.

C.3.2.2.1.5   Capacitance-change devices

Unlike light-change devices, capacitance-change devices are not likely to be suspected by criminals, and the thing detected, or capacitance, is invisible. This means that intruders are less likely to avoid such devices.

Capacitance-change devices are based on the fact that under stable conditions, electrostatic charges (the same static electricity that is responsible for electric shocks common in dry climates when someone touches a doorknob after walking across a carpet) are balanced between masses of metal, or antennas, and the earth's potential. These charges are influenced by nearby movement even if conditions are not suitable for a spark to fly. Changes in this stable capacitance can be detected and used as one element of an electronic circuit in such a way that if the potential is disturbed, as it would be by an intruder's presence, an alarm will be sounded.

C.3.2.2.1.6   Sound detectors

Just as sound striking a microphone can generate sufficient electrical current after suitable amplification to be recorded or broadcast, such electricity may be used to trigger an alarm. Of course, care must be taken to obtain the proper tradeoff between sensitivity and rejection of false alarms. Sound alarms are often combined with sound recorders.

C.3.2.2.2   Active systems

While passive systems do not radiate energy, active systems do. Such energy can take the form of sound waves or electromagnetic signals.

C.3.2.2.2.1   Sonic motion detectors

Sonic motion detectors consist of a transmitter that radiates sound waves and a detector that receives them. The sound used is generally of a frequency high enough not to be normally detectable by humans; therefore, the systems are often called ultrasonic motion detectors. When the receiver or receivers and transmitter are operating in a balanced mode, no alarm is generated, but a change in the reception pattern caused by a body moving in a protected area causes a disturbance in the reception pattern. When this happens, a voltage change is generated and an alarm triggered.

C.3.2.2.2.2   Microwave motion detectors

Whereas sonic detectors are similar in operation to radar units, microwave motion detectors *are* radar units of a primitive and limited kind. Their principles of operation are much the same as their sonic cousins, except that radio, or electromagnetic, waves are used instead of sound waves. (See figure 8.)

C.3.2.3   Fire detection

Libraries use various fire detection methods. Probably the most common are smoke detectors (both optical and by detecting the ionized

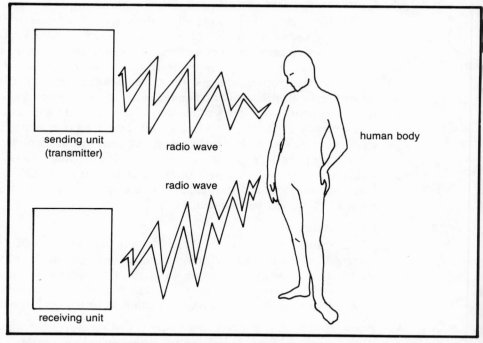

sending unit
(transmitter)

radio wave

human body

radio wave

receiving unit

Fig. 8. Motion detection. Radio waves bounce off the human body and signal the receiving unit.

particles present in smoke) and temperature sensors (both absolute and rate-of-change).

C.3.2.4   Water detection

While fire is the more obvious danger for libraries, water damage is often a greater risk. Water damage may result from leaky roofs, fire control systems, or even clogged plumbing.

There are two common methods of detecting unwanted water: the float method and the electronic method.

C.3.2.4.1   Float detection

In this technique, a sump is dug at the lowest point in a building or at other points where water is likely to accumulate. In this sump is placed a float, which is attached to a switch. If sufficient water enters the sump to cause the float to rise, the switch closes and activates an alarm. This same principle shuts off flush toilets and may also activate a pump to remove the water.

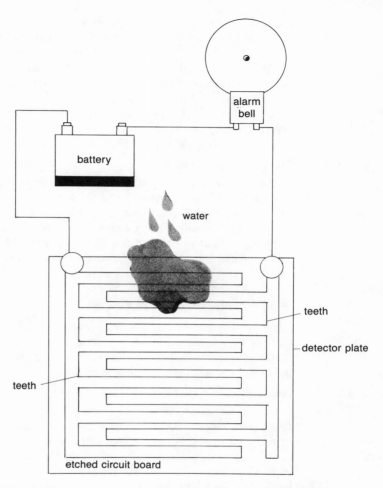

Fig. 9. Water detection. The detector plate is made up of interlocking but not touching "teeth." When water bridges the teeth, a circuit is completed.

C.3.2.4.2   Electronic detection

Water in smaller amounts can be detected using a wire or foil grid. Presence of water or water vapor changes the conductance and capacitance of such a grid. This change can then be linked to an alarm circuit. (See figure 9.)

C.3.2.5   Other

The potential problems of libraries (noxious chemicals and gases, temperature, lightning, and so on) are manifold, and each has its technology of detection. In nearly every case, however, detection techniques are divided, as in the examples above, between passive and active sensors, with both techniques depending on some change influencing a balanced electronic circuit or activating a simple switch.

One more general security consideration that has great impact on all the above is often overlooked: electricity. Virtually all the security devices described above depend on electricity to function. In order to make security technology failsafe, every system should include a power failure detector. Without this detector, any security device can be rendered inoperable by the very problems it was intended to detect.

C.3.3   **Security notification**

Despite the technology that makes capacitative-difference or radar detection possible, an alarm must be received by the appropriate party in order to be useful. Such notice should be automatic (using preprogrammed telephone dialing technology or direct lines to appropriate agencies such as police and fire departments) and should include the failsafe techniques mentioned above to ensure that failure of a notification circuit itself causes an alarm.

C.4   **Mechanical data storage and retrieval**

Although mechanical data storage and retrieval are often considered to have been replaced by electronic methods, a large amount of such media is still in use. For this reason, and because of its historical importance, the discussion below is included.

C.4.1   **Hollerith card–based systems**

Once the standard method of storing programs and data, Hollerith cards (also called IBM cards and tabulating cards) have been largely superseded by other media. An outgrowth of the original punched card developed by Herman Hollerith for the United States Census Bureau, Hollerith cards were standardized into the current form of 3-1/4 by 7-1/4 inches. This size was selected because it matched that of the dollar bill then in use and therefore could use already existing storage and handling equipment.

C.4.1.1   Storage techniques

Data are stored on Hollerith cards by encoding letters, numbers, and other characters into the presence or absence of rectangular holes in predetermined columns. There are positions for eighty such columns on a standard card. Each column can have punches in twelve positions. The top two positions are called the 11 and 12 zones, and the bottom ten are the 0 to 9 positions. Digits are encoded using a single punch in the 0 to 9 positions, while letters require two punches: one in the 0 position or 11 or 12 zone, and another in a (1–9) digit position. Punctuation and special characters generally require three punches per column. (See figure 10.)

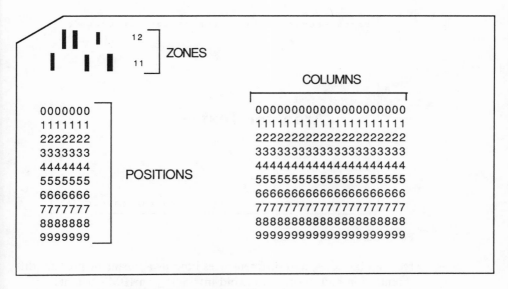

Fig. 10. Elements of a Hollerith card

C.4.1.2   Devices used

Data are encoded into Hollerith cards by a keypunch machine. Such a machine accepts input from a typewriterlike keyboard and punches the proper hole or holes in a given column, optionally printing the corresponding character at the top of the column. Provision is also made for reproducing existing cards and for interpreting cards (printing characters corresponding to encoded data when this was not done at the time of production). The most common situation resulting in such uninterpreted cards is when they are produced as computer output.

Data on the cards are read using a card reader. A hole is sensed by electromechanical brushes or light transmission, and these binary (hole/no-hole) data are converted into electrical signals for use by a computer or other device.

While in later years Hollerith cards were most commonly used as computer input and output media, a variety of noncomputerized machinery was also available for their use. In fact, for many years after the cards' invention, computers did not exist. Mechanical sorters, tabulators, and collators were the primary users of such cards during the time between the cards' invention around the turn of the century and the advent of the computer in the 1950s.

The Hollerith card, although the most common punched card format, was not unique. Other manufacturers introduced a variety of formats using such modifications as multiple columns, round rather than

107

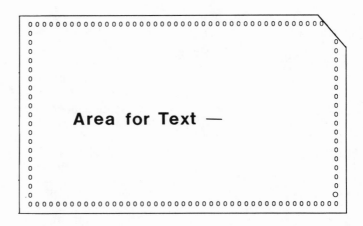

Fig. 11. Edge-notched card

rectangular holes, and different sizes both as a means of product differentiation and in order to avoid infringing on IBM's patents.

This mechanical encoding and sorting technology is still used in conjunction with microforms in the aperture card. In this system, an image of an architectural drawing, for example, is produced on film and mounted in a cutout on a Hollerith card. This obviously reduces the amount of data that can be stored on the card, since the columns that correspond to the filmchip's location cannot be used, but it allows fast sorting and retrieval of the document on the film.

C.4.1.3   Library uses

In addition to storage and retrieval of images using aperture cards by special libraries, Hollerith card technology was used extensively in library circulation, bookkeeping, and serials check-in systems. All systems that use Hollerith cards suffered from the problems of bulk, the difficulty in making changes, the inherent batch nature of such operations, and the small amount of data that could be encoded on a single card.

C.4.2   Edge-notched cards

Unlike Hollerith cards, which are commonly used in conjunction with computers, edge-notched cards are manipulated using only the simplest of tools. The cards themselves are sheets of stock in various sizes, although cards to be used together must be the same size. They are manufactured under a variety of names, including handsort cards, marginal-hole punch cards, and Keysort Cards, a trademark of the McBee Corporation.

Regardless of size, edge-notched cards consist of a central open area for writing or typing data and a series of holes drilled around the periphery of the card for mechanical data encoding. (See figure 11.)

C.4.2.1   Storage techniques

Data are coded by notching the card, that is, by cutting away the portion of the card between the hole and the card edge. This results in producing an indentation rather than an actual hole in the card. This form of mutilation is binary in nature: either there is a hole present or there is a notch.

In the technique's simplest form, yes or no data or other binary data such as male or female, or adult or juvenile can be encoded directly; that is, for binary data, the data element to hole ratio is 1. A set of holes could be used for example, to record the language or languages used in a document; each language represented would have its corresponding hole notched out. Thus, when searching for documents in Urdu, a researcher need look only for cards with the Urdu hole notched and retrieve the documents such cards represent.

More complex data can be encoded at the expense of the data element to hole ratio by using sections of the card to represent letters or other data. For example, digits from 0 to 9 can be encoded unambiguously using groups of six holes:

```
    0    0  0  0  0  0
   S-D   7  4  2  1  0
```

The S-D notation stands for single digit. To code the digit 6, the 4 and 2 holes would be notched; to code a 3, the 2 and 1 holes; and to code a 7, the S-D and 7 holes. Thus, each digit can be coded as a set of exactly two notches out of the six. This saves four holes if a person wants to encode the digits from 0 to 9, at a cost of requiring twice as much searching (since to search for the 7 requires a search for both 7 and S-D, and to search for a 3 requires a search for both the 2 and 1). This is not a particularly good tradeoff, but if a person wishes to code one hundred possibilities from 0 to 99, he or she need use only twelve holes, coding the first digit in the first six holes and the second digit in the second six. Thus, a person must search for four notches but use only twelve rather than one hundred holes, a much better tradeoff. Of course, this same technique can be used for larger numbers by increasing one set of six holes for each additional digit.

A slightly more complicated coding scheme called a pyramid code can reduce the number of holes needed for a digit to only five. In this code, a grid or pyramid of digits is printed on the card:

```
   0  0  0  0  0
    9  5  2  0
     8  4  1
      7  3
       6
```

Digits are coded by selecting the digit in the pyramid and then follow-ing along the two diagonals leading from it in order to select the two proper holes to notch. Thus a 3 is coded:

```
0  U  0  0  U
  9  5  2  0
    8  4  1
      7  3
        6
```

and a 2 is coded:

```
0  0  U  U  0
  9  5  2  0
    8  4  1
      7  3
        6
```

Alphabetic data can also be coded. In fact, letters can be unambigu-ously coded using only five holes with a maximum of four searches per letter:

```
  0    0  0  0  0
N–Z  7  4  2  1
```

In this scheme, the N–Z hole is notched only if the letter to be encoded falls in the second half of the alphabet. Thus, using the code A = 1, B = 2, and so on to Z = 13 (plus N–Z), the entire alphabet can be en-coded:

```
A  B  C  D  E  F  G  H  I  J  K  L  M
1  2  3  4  5  6  7  8  9  10 11 12 13
N  O  P  Q  R  S  T  U  V  W  X  Y  Z
```

The N–Z hole must be notched for the bottom row.

Using this code, a K (number 11) is encoded by notching the 7 and 4 holes; an N (number 1 in the N–Z row) by notching the 1 and N–Z holes; a B by notching only the 2 hole; and a Z by notching the 7, 4, 2, and N–Z holes. Such a code is exceptionally cumbersome to use for long words.

This difficulty may be partially overcome at the cost of a secondary look-up by using fields with an index either printed on the card or in a separate document. Thus, assuming a person wished to encode only a single term in each set of holes, 1,000 terms could be coded by assign-ing each term a number from 000 to 999 and then notching three sets of 5 holes using a pyramid code.

It is even possible at the expense of increased noise and erroneous retrieval to encode more subjects than there are holes by using various random number coding schemes.

C.4.2.2   Devices used

Edge-notched cards are coded by using a notcher to change a hole into a notch. Notchers look and operate like a notebook hole punch or a train conductor's ticket punch. When it is necessary to code a large number of cards with the same data (as when recording a date of matriculation for a class), a groover, which is simply a larger version of a notcher capable of notching more than one card at a time, is used.

Detection of encoded data by their notches is accomplished by means of a sorting needle. This is a thin rod much like a knitting needle with a handle. To retrieve all cards with a notch in a given location, the rod is passed through the entire deck of cards and raised. Those with the hole notched out, that is, with the data coded, drop out, and those that are not coded hang on the needle. Of course, if digits, letters, or more complex codes are used, the needling must be inserted more than once.

Incidentally, when using such a mechanical storage and retrieval technique, the term "false drop," often used in an abstract sense with newer technology, takes on a concrete meaning.

C.4.2.3   Library uses

Before the availability of microcomputers, libraries often used edge-notched cards for circulation systems and patron registration. Such systems are still in use and provide good service with relatively low continuing costs. While few libraries would select this system today, the value of such techniques is high enough that many libraries continue to use them rather than convert to computers.

C.4.3   **Optical systems**

Before today's almost universal availability of computers, a common problem of information storage and retrieval facilities, including libraries, was conducting logical searches. One need only consider the difficulties of a card catalog search for books dealing with Hawaii's or Guam's tourist or convention industry that are not published by governments or universities, for example, to appreciate the need for alternative techniques. Both Hollerith card and edge-notched card systems are limited by the number of holes that can be contained on a given card. Both are essentially document systems where a card represents a document, and various attributes of the document are coded on it. Such techniques allow only limited numbers of attributes to be coded unless libraries can tolerate severe problems.

Optical storage and retrieval systems were developed as mirror images of such document-based systems, being instead aspect-based systems. In these systems, a card or other storage device represents a single aspect, attribute, concept, or subject, and document numbers are recorded on it. Such schemes require an additional look-up step because when appropriate document numbers are retrieved, they must be translated into bibliographic data; however, this shortcoming is often less important than the value of being able to perform logical searches.

The storage medium itself may be of various materials (sheets of paper, cardstock, photographic film, or even thin metal strips) and of various sizes. Because of this diversity of materials, this discussion has settled on the term "card" to represent any such storage unit. When the word "card" is used, the reader should take it to mean any of the many forms of recording media. Of course, searches must be done using media of the same type and size.

C.4.3.1 Storage techniques

In general, optical systems use holes to represent document numbers. These numbers are coded by position; that is, the first position on each card represents document number one, the second represents document number two, and so on.

Normally, each card represents a different aspect of the materials to be indexed. One card might represent Hawaii, for instance; a second, Guam. Documents that contain information about these places would be coded on the card by punching out the position representing the document's number. Logical Boolean *and* searches can be accomplished by superimposing the cards representing the terms desired. Positions that represent documents sharing these terms allow light to pass; documents not sharing the terms block the light. This basic search technique explains the alternative names for this storage technology: the peek-a-boo card and the optical stencil. (See figure 12.)

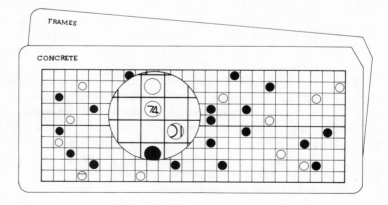

Fig. 12. Optical storage card

C.4.3.2   Devices used

In their simplest form, devices need only be hand punches to make holes at the document number sites, but quite elaborate machinery for using this technique was developed in the era before computers became common. Such machinery allowed as many as 10,000 documents to be coded onto each card.

C.4.3.3   Library uses

Optical storage and retrieval systems were used primarily in large special libraries, especially in government and private research and development facilities. They normally indexed documents rather than books and were never common in more general-purpose libraries. Nonetheless, optical storage and retrieval systems were important forms of technology in their time and like edge-notched and Hollerith cards are completely analogous to many electronic techniques now used in computer-assisted information storage and retrieval. Indeed, many limitations that seem illogical to new professionals, such as the eighty columns commonly displayed on terminals, can be traced directly back to the physical limitations of these early storage and retrieval devices.

C.5   **Computers**

In a general sense, computers help transform data into information. They accept data from the outside world, process that data into a useful form, and then, perhaps after storing it temporarily, make the resulting information available once again to the outside world. The term "computer" has undergone a shift in meaning from a person who computes, to a person using a machine and performing computations, to the machine that performs the computations.

C.5.1   **Analog**

Analog computers solve problems by manipulating continuous variables that represent data. An example of an analog computer familiar to most people is the slide rule. Slide rules use length or distance to represent the numbers in problems; more commonly, analog computers use electricity. In any case, they operate by measuring something that represents the appropriate quantities.

Analog computers were once known as scientific computers because they were the preferred form of technology for the continuous variables (temperature, flow, speed, and so on) found in scientific problems. Before the explosive development of digital computers in the 1950s and 1960s, analog computers were considered the best available technology for engineering and science but have been largely but not completely superseded by digital units.

C.5.2 **Digital**

Where analog computers deal with continuous quantities, digital computers work with discrete quantities. They operate by counting and performing logic rather than by measuring and are thus particularly well suited for working with things that exist in discrete amounts, such as money. Continuous variables must be transformed into a series of discrete measures before computations can be performed on such data.

While digital computers have used various technologies for counting, modern machines almost universally are electronic, using electricity to represent the quantities they manipulate. Because digital computers are the only type of computer librarians are likely to encounter, the term "computer" in this discussion should be taken to mean electronic digital computer.

C.5.2.1 Components

A computer, as the term is commonly used, is actually a system made up of several parts. This makeup, or architecture, is consistent across computer types and sizes. The system is composed of sections (which may be individual components or subsystems): input and output devices get data into and out of the computer; memory devices store data; and the central processing unit (CPU) processes the data into information. Other noncentral parts are often called peripheral devices or just peripherals.

C.5.2.1.1 Input and output

While some devices such as keyboards are used only for inputting data, and others such as printers are used only for output, many input and output devices are similar, if not identical.

C.5.2.1.1.1 Input units

Data input to computers must be digital and electronic in nature, and there are a variety of devices that produce such data. The simplest of these consists of just a bank of switches that can be set by the computer operator to represent letters, numbers, and instructions. This arrangement was used both for the earliest operational computers such as ENIAC and for the first personal computers.

This form of input was extremely tedious to use though, and improved methods of input were soon devised. Binary systems already in use, including teletypes (TTYs), Hollerith card readers, and paper tape, were adapted. Of these, only the teletype, which looked much like an electric typewriter, was directly connected to the computer. Pressing a key resulted in both a typed character for human use and an electrical signal for computer use. Hollerith card and paper tape input required a two-step process. Using the appropriate punching device, an operator prepared cards or tape representing data in binary form. This medium was then fed into a card or tape reader that converted the punches to electrical signals.

A more common form of input today is a refinement of the teletype: the terminal. This device, which may be either printing or screen based, consists of a keyboard, a display device, and the necessary encoding circuitry to produce signals appropriate to the computer. Terminals that produce printed copy are commonly still referred to as TTYs, while those with television, or cathode ray tube, displays are usually called cathode ray terminals (CRTs), video display terminals (VDTs), or video display units (VDUs). One complication is that for microcomputer systems, there are three common types of VDUs, differentiated by the signals sent to them. One VDU accepts a signal like that a television tuner sends to a television set: composite video. This signal may deliver either color or black and white images. The second kind of VDU accepts digital signals and is called TTL (for transistor to transistor logic), a term used to describe the type of integrated circuits now used by most computers. The third VDU is called RGB (for red, green, blue) since it accepts signals representing these three colors. In addition to these fundamental VDU types, there are several levels of image and color quality. The different types of displays are not interchangeable and must be matched with the computer's output circuits. To allow displays to be changed, such circuitry is often on plug-in cards.

In addition to these devices, which are generally used only for input or output, many storage devices, such as tape and disk, may also be used for input and output operations.

C.5.2.1.1.2 Output units

All input devices and media described above with the exception of switches may also be used for output. Thus, a computer may be connected to a CRT, a TTY, or a card punch for output. As mentioned above, however, there are devices used solely for output: printers.

Printers convert electrical signals from computers to printed characters. Of course, a TTY also can do this; the difference is that while a TTY may be used for input, a printer may not. Printers are most easily described in terms of the quantity of print they produce at one time: characters, lines, or pages.

C.5.2.1.1.2.1 Character printers

Character printers print one character at a time. Usually they are capable of producing eighty standard columns in a line, although some can use wider paper to print more columns, or can compress their print in order to print more characters in a given space. Some units move paper through the printer by friction, just like standard typewriters; others use tractor mechanisms, feeding paper by using pins that fit into corresponding holes along the paper's edge to pull the often continuous paper through. Some units use both forms of paper advance.

C.5.2.1.1.2.1.1   Formed character printers

Formed character printers may be thought of as typewriter technology attached to a computer. As such, any of the electric typewriter type elements, for example, the typebar, ball element, daisywheel, or print thimble, may be used. Such printers are characterized by the attractive hand-typed appearance of their output and, except for typebar units, by their ability to change type fonts by switching the type elements. They also tend to be expensive, slow (fifteen to fifty characters per second), and because of the impact of their elements striking the paper, noisy.

C.5.2.1.1.2.1.2   Dot matrix printers

Dot matrix printers use a grid of dots to form letters. Thus, the letter "l" may consist of a vertical line of dots. The actual print may be produced either through mechanical means, with pins representing the appropriate dots being pushed against a ribbon, or thermally, with "hot spots" representing the appropriate dots being created electrically to change the color of special paper. Other types of dot matrix printers include inkjet and electrostatic printers.

Dot matrix print varies greatly in quality, generally depending on the number of dots that make up a character. The most common grid size is seven by nine dots, although this standard is now being exceeded in newer units. At their best, high-density dot matrix printers approach formed character print quality, but improvements in print quality are made at the expense of increased cost and decreased speed.

Dot matrix printers are generally faster than formed character printers, producing 50 to 350 characters per second, are quieter and often less expensive, and provide a variety of fonts and graphics; however, print quality is usually inferior.

C.5.2.1.1.2.2   Line printers

Line printers print a full line at a time. They are impact printers that use either bands or a belt, also called a chain or train, of characters. When the appropriate characters are set, which may be thought of as being done simultaneously for all characters making up a line, a hammer pushes the paper against the characters through an intervening ribbon. Line printers are expensive and are generally restricted to use with mainframe and minicomputers but are fast, producing up to 2,000 132-character lines per minute. Their print quality is not as good as single formed character print but similar in quality to mediocre dot matrix print (although not in form since line printers use formed characters).

C.5.2.1.1.2.3 Page printers

Page printers, also called laser printers, use the same technology as xerographic copiers except that the image on the charged drum is produced not photographically but by directing a laser beam. This beam is itself controlled using microcomputer technology and technically could be thought of as dot matrix since the characters are produced by discrete charged spots on the drum. The number of dots is high, however, and the melting of the toner produces an additional smoothing effect so that, to the naked eye, the finished characters look almost typeset.

Laser printers are quiet and relatively fast. For units designed for connection to microcomputers, plain typescript takes about ten seconds per page regardless of the amount of type on it. In actual use, however, additional graphics elements or multiple type fonts can increase this time dramatically. Laser printers are capable of producing high-quality graphics material and are surprisingly inexpensive, costing about as much as a high-quality formed character printer. Laser printers designed for connection to mainframe and minicomputers are both much more expensive and much faster, producing as many as 300 pages per minute.

C.5.2.1.2   Central processing unit

The central processing unit (CPU) is often described as the brain or heart of a computer. It comprises three parts: the control unit, the arithmetic and logic unit (ALU), and the main, primary memory. These parts may be physically located in one, two, or more units but are conceptually separate in any case. Often the ALU and control unit are considered together as a processor unit.

C.5.2.1.2.1   Control unit

The control unit directs the flow of data to and from memory, the ALU, and input and output circuits. This flow occurs over sets of wires called busses and is synchronized with the needs of various computer parts through a series of pulses from a crystal controlled clock. Clearly, the faster this clock runs, within the capabilities of the circuits involved, the more the computer can accomplish in a given amount of time. Clock speeds commonly encountered in microcomputers vary from about 1 million cycles per second, or 1 MHz, to about 15 MHz, and speeds of as much as 25 MHz are being used. Minicomputers and mainframes often operate faster—some faster than 30 MHz.

C.5.2.1.2.2   Arithmetic and logic unit

The arithmetic and logic unit accepts data sent by the control unit, temporarily stores it in registers, and then performs operations on it as directed by the control unit. Such operations take two basic forms: arithmetic and logical. Arithmetic operations generally consist of add-

117

ing, subtracting, multiplying, or dividing two numbers stored in registers and then putting the result in a register. This result can then be transferred by the control unit either to memory or to an output device.

When performing logic operations, the ALU compares numbers in two registers and then reports to the control unit whether they are the same or whether one is larger or smaller than the other.

C.5.2.1.2.3 Memory

A computer's main memory stores data being used for processing. Computer memory may be conceptualized as a series of numbered pigeonholes each of which can generally store one character, such as a letter or number. The control unit keeps track of what is stored where and directs its transfer as needed.

Many forms of main memory have been used in computers. Until recently, the standard was core storage, a technique developed in the early 1950s that used small toroids, or doughnut-shaped pieces, of an iron-based, or ferric, material. These individual toroids could be magnetized to represent the individual binary digits to be stored. While this technology is not used in new computers, many operational units have such memory, and main computer memories that use other techniques are still sometimes referred to as core memory.

A more recent and more common form of memory uses integrated circuits on silicon chips to store data. These devices may either be permanently filled with data (read-only memory, or ROM), or the storage locations may be able to be used over and over (random-access memory, or RAM). Microcomputers commonly use both types: ROM to store programs and data that will remain constant, RAM to store temporary data or programs. The difference between the two from an operational standpoint is that when a computer is turned off, RAM is erased, but data in ROM are still present when the machine is turned on again. In an attempt to overcome this weakness, some computers use battery power to retain still-useful RAM memory when the computer is turned off.

Microcomputers are often described in terms of the amount of main memory they possess: a 64K machine has about 64,000 storage locations, a 512K machine about 512,000 storage locations, and a 2M unit about 2 million.

C.5.2.1.3 External storage

While the RAM in a computer's main storage can be quickly accessed by the control unit, it has several drawbacks. First, as stated above, when the machine is turned off, data stored in RAM disappears. Interestingly, although this is true for modern machines using integrated-circuit RAM, it was not true of the now outmoded ferric core units. Second, RAM's available storage is limited. A book, for example,

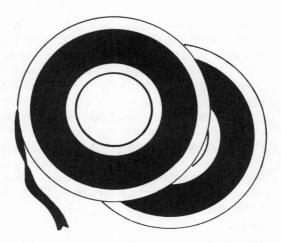

Fig. 13. Computer tape

could not be stored in 64K of main memory even if the machine was never turned off; it is just too big to fit. It would also be inconvenient to try to move data stored in RAM from one machine to another; the two units would have to be physically connected.

External memory overcomes these disadvantages: it is more permanent and generally holds more data; however, it takes the control unit longer to access it. While Hollerith cards were at one time the most common external storage medium, magnetic storage is now almost universal. This storage takes the form of tape or disks. In both forms of storage, data are represented by magnetic spots recorded in meaningful patterns on a metallic coating on a substrate.

C.5.2.1.3.1   Tape

Computer tape is much like tape used for audio recordings and may be enclosed in cassettes or spooled on open reels. (See figure 13.) It is available in various lengths and widths. Data are recorded on the tape using recording heads much like those on audio recorders.

In mainframes and minicomputers, several recording heads are stacked in a computer tape unit so that the individual binary digits that represent a character as well as certain error-checking, or parity, data may be recorded simultaneously in a column. Each of these recording heads records a separate track, and one of the parameters used to specify tape drives and recorded tape is the number of tracks. Tape units also vary in the number of characters they record per inch, that is, they vary in density, measured in bytes per inch, or bpi. Tape is a relatively dense storage medium; a tape of typical length, using common recording parameters, may approach a storage capacity of 50 million characters.

Microcomputers generally use a different storage technique to record on tape, one in which digital data are used to modulate an audio signal. This signal is then recorded using normal audio techniques. Such computers ordinarily use stock tape cassette units, although cassette recorders that have been optimized for computer use are available.

One important feature of tape is that it is inherently a sequential medium. That is, in order to move to any record, a person must first scan past all preceding records. While there have been some ingenious attempts to minimize the problems this causes, tape or other serial media is generally most useful when individual records do not need to be updated often and when a large proportion of the entire file will be processed at one time.

C.5.2.1.3.2 Disks

Disk storage is much like tape storage in that it records data magnetically. It differs, though, in several important respects. First, rather than all binary digits that represent a character being written at one time, or in parallel, disk storage writes the bits one after the other, or serially.

A second major difference is that while tape is a sequential medium, disks, although they can be used sequentially, are capable of direct access. In direct access, an individual record may be reached without first scanning past all preceding records. In this respect, computer disks are much like audio disks in that a person can move directly to the recording desired.

Floppy disks and their associated disk drives are relatively rugged and inexpensive, but the more expensive and fragile hard disks can hold more information and access it faster. Floppy drives rotate at about 300 revolutions per minute while hard disks rotate about ten times faster. Mainframe computers normally use hard disks exclusively while minicomputers and microcomputers may be equipped with either or both.

Recently, there has been much interest in storage using nonmagnetic means. Various forms of optical disks are currently available, although magnetic storage on tapes and disks remains more common.

C.5.2.1.3.2.1 Floppy disks

Floppy disks, also called flexible disks or diskettes, are constructed of the same material used in magnetic tape and are shaped like very flat doughnuts. They come in several sizes, most commonly 8, 5^1/$_4$, and 3^1/$_2$ inches in diameter. The disk drive, the device used to read and write disks, consists of a motor that turns a spindle that in turn engages both the central hole on the disk and a movable read and write head that touches the disk. This head is moved in discrete steps across the spinning disk to access tracks upon which data are recorded. The entire disk is covered by a plastic jacket that has holes cut out for access by the spindle and the read and write head; the jacket also has an index hole used to indicate the beginning of the tracks. Most 5¹/₄- and 8-inch disks also have a small rectangular notch cut out of one side of the jacket. A microswitch in the disk drive determines whether the disk can be recorded based on whether the notch is present. A small piece of tape can be used to cover this notch and prevent or allow recording. Smaller 3¹/₂-inch disks are enclosed in more robust packages and use a sliding piece of plastic to prevent recording. Some disk drives contain only a single head and therefore read and write only one side of a disk while others use two heads, one for each side, thus doubling the disk's capacity. (See figure 14.)

It is important to realize that while each size disk works only with its corresponding drive, a disk's recording density, number of tracks, and number of sides are determined by the disk drive, not the disk. Disks are available in various combinations of density, tracks, and sides, but this designation refers only to the level at which the disks were tested and certified; there is little difference between disks beyond the testing and guarantee.

Data are stored on disks in tracks produced by the discrete movement of the head in and out across the disk. Floppy disk drives vary in the number of tracks they use, but figures from about 30 to 120 tracks per side have been cited for various computers. Data are stored within a track in sectors defined in relation to an index hole or to a special electronic mark on the disk; the number of sectors per track varies from machine to machine. These variations are one reason disks recorded on a computer of one type often cannot be read by another computer of a different type.

C.5.2.1.3.2.2 Hard disks

Mainframe computers use hard disks almost exclusively while minicomputers and microcomputers are also commonly equipped with hard disks. While hard disks are conceptually much the same as floppy units, there are several practical differences. First, they rotate much faster. Second, the read and write head does not actually touch the surface of the hard disk because it is kept away by the force of the air caused by the disk's rotation. Should the head touch the surface of a rotating hard disk, a head crash results with the head scraping away at the magnetic material and destroying the data and often the head.

Hard disks are often stacked into disk packs. These packs are used in disk drives with the appropriate number of read and write heads to increase the storage available. Some units can store over 300 million characters, or 300 megabytes.

Hard disks may be either removable or nonremovable (fixed). Hard disks for microcomputers are generally fixed and are sometimes called

Winchesters. Such drives now commonly store up to about 80 megabytes, but this will probably increase. (See figure 15.)

C.5.2.1.3.2.3 Optical storage

There are three forms of optical storage currently in use as computer media: the compact disk–read-only memory (referred to universally as CD-ROM), the video disk, and the optical digital disk. All three use laser technology to read and write data, although CD-ROM disks are currently the most common.

CD-ROM disks are similar to digital compact audio disks (see C.7.2.1.3). They can hold as much as 550 megabytes of data, use sophisticated error detection and correction devices that make them virtually error free, and are already becoming common for such tasks as storing bibliographic citations or MARC records for local library searching.

Video disks record individual frames in an analog fashion, and while they are most commonly used to record television images for use in training or home entertainment, the same technology could be used to record data for library use. Video disks store about 54,000 images per disk.

Optical digital disks operate by burning discrete marks in a substrate, the same recording technique used for CD-ROM disks. As such, it is analogous to magnetic recording. Optical digital disks are less common now than CD-ROM disks but probably hold as much potential for library applications because, of the three formats, only optical

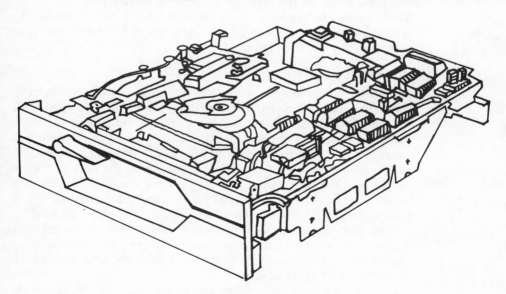

Fig. 14. Floppy disk drive mechanism

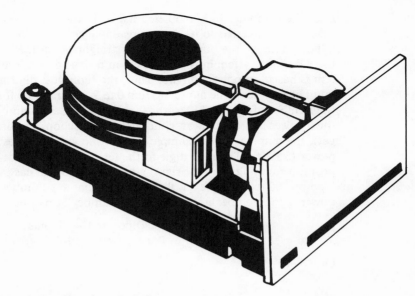

Fig. 15. Hard disk drive mechanism (protective covering removed)

digital disks may be easily written at local sites. Both CD-ROM and video disks are more suitable for studio mastering and reproduction. However, optical digital disks do share with the other formats the characteristic of permanence: once data are written, they cannot be deleted or changed.

Thus, while all three optical formats may be and often are produced from a master copy and distributed, optical digital disks are also commonly written in the field. Technology for writing CD-ROM disks is also becoming available to individual users, but video disks are almost always studio produced. In any case, writing is permanent; it may be added to but not deleted or changed. When data deletion or change is needed, a new copy is made and the old is retained. This characteristic has given these units the name of WORM (write once, read mostly) technology.

C.5.2.2   Data representation

Computers are inherently binary in nature; a switch is either open or closed, a magnetic spot is present or it is not. Humans, on the other hand, use ten digits, more than twenty letters, and many special symbols. These digits, letters, and symbols must be read and recorded by the computer using only binary representation. This is accomplished by coding the human characters. Each character uses more space in binary form but is able to be manipulated by the computer. Of course,

123

once the computer has completed its work, the binary representation must be reconverted to its human-readable counterpart.

For numbers, the binary system is straightforward. Where humans use a decimal system normally based on powers of ten, the binary system is based on powers of two. Thus, the rightmost digit in a decimal number represents the numbers from 0 to 9—or, in more formal terms, the number of cases of 10 to the 0 power. Since any number raised to the 0 power is 1 (a fact most children learn in school and promptly forget), the number 5, for example, can be shown as 5 times 10 to the 0 power (5×10^0). The next digit to the left in a number, or the second position counting from the right, gives the number of cases of 10 to the 1 power (00 to 90) since another rule says that any number to the first power is the number itself. Thus, the number 51 can be shown:

$$1 \text{ times } 10 \text{ to the } 0 \text{ power } 1 \times 10^0 \text{ plus}$$
$$5 \text{ times } 10 \text{ to the } 1 \text{ power } 5 \times 10^1$$

Or,   10
         10
         10
         10
         10
        +1
        ——
         51

A number's third column from the right gives the number of cases of 10 to the 2 power (10^2), 000 to 900. The number 765 is made up of 7 times 10^2, plus 6 times 10^1, plus 5 time 10^0. The number 105 is broken down as one case of 1 times 10^2, no cases of 10^1, and five cases of 10^0.

The binary system works the same way but uses only the digits 0 and 1. The rightmost digit is the number of cases of 2^0 (0 to 1), the next left digit represents the number of cases of 2^1 (0 to 2), the next left 2^2 (0 to 4), and so on. The binary number 1010 is made of 1 case of 2^3 (decimal 8) plus 1 case of 2^1 (decimal 2). There are no cases of 2^0 or 2^2. Therefore, binary 1010 is equivalent to the decimal value of 10, or:

1 times 2^3	8
0 times 2^2	0
1 times 2^1	2
0 times 2^0	+0
	10

Because people often find binary representation confusing and computers cannot easily deal with any other system, two other systems that can easily be converted between the two are common: octal and hexadecimal, or hex. Octal uses powers of base 8, and hexadecimal uses powers of base 16. These systems are used because each produces a number where a constant number of binary digits is represented by each octal or hexadecimal digit. Thus, the binary number 1111 (decimal 15) is represented by a single hex character. Unfortunately, hex needs sixteen digits—0 through 9 plus six more. The letters A through F are used for this purpose; therefore, binary 1111 is hex F. Hex and octal systems allow humans to directly specify or be told the binary content of storage locations without the tedious translation of 0s and 1s. By convention, hex numbers are preceded by a dollar sign; thus, decimal value 15 would normally be written $F in hex.

Representing letters and other symbols requires that an additional digit be added to signal that the code is not a number. The two most common letter and symbol coding schemes are EBCDIC (Extended Binary Coded Decimal Interchange Code), used for some medium and large computers, especially IBM units, and ASCII (American Standard Code for Information Interchange), used in almost all microcomputers and many medium and large computers.

Within a computer, characters are stored in eight bit units called bytes. Most commonly, a byte represents a single character, although each character needs only seven bits, as explained in C.2.1.2. The eighth bit, a parity bit, can be used for error checking or can be used along with the other seven bits to encode special characters, diacritics, or graphics elements. Unlike the seven bits that make up the ASCII character set (see C.2.1.2), these extended characters are not standardized. Occasionally, computers make use of four-bit, or half-byte, unit called a nybble.

C.5.2.3   Construction generations

Certain technical advances led to rapid spurts of computer development. It has become traditional to refer to these levels of development in terms of generations. The first generation is represented by those early computers such as ENIAC and Whirlwind that used vacuum tubes as their basic building blocks. Second generation computers such as the IBM 1620 used transistors. The third generation, represented by most microcomputers and minicomputers such as the DEC VAX, used integrated circuits that combined many transistors on a single chip. The fourth generation includes today's most advanced computers and uses very large-scale integration (VLSI) technology to combine the functions of many integrated circuits on a single chip. (See figure 16.)

As the generations advanced, computers became easier to use, faster, smaller, and (for a given computing power), "smarter." The projected fifth and sixth generation computers carry this one step further with technology supporting a computer that possesses true artificial intelligence.

C.5.2.4   Marketing types

Computers range from small hand-held units to gigantic supercompu-
ters. While all may be quite similar in their basic building blocks, they
are commonly used for different purposes and often have different re-

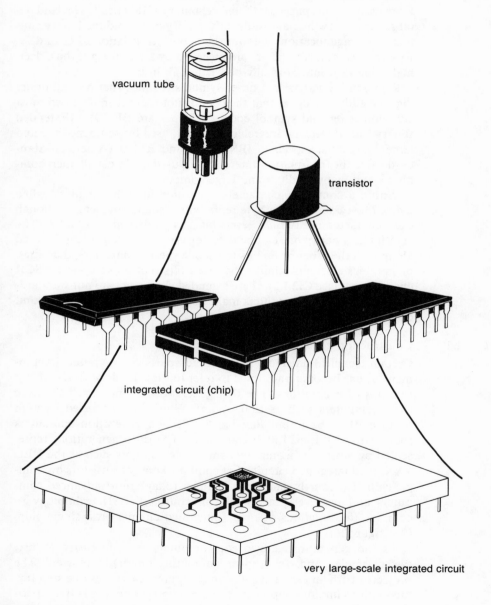

Fig. 16. Construction generations

quirements for environment and staff. A series of terms describing various computer types has evolved; while having no official definitions, the terms are understood and propagated by persons working with computers. Some of these terms have been listed below. It is important to realize that these are basically marketing terms or jargon, and as such defy precise definition. They also have been used by some companies or individuals to obscure differences as well as to point them out. Nonetheless, librarians must be aware of the terms' more common usages.

C.5.2.4.1   Mainframes

Mainframe computers are large in size, are commonly owned by large organizations, cost a large amount of money (over $250,000), and have large computing capacities. They usually require special environmental conditions such as air conditioning and purification and therefore are normally housed in special facilities with special staffs responsible only for them. Commonly, mainframes comprise several physical units and can although often do not support a great many remote input and output devices. Often an organization will have only one mainframe.

C.5.2.4.2   Minicomputers

Minicomputers are generally less expensive than mainframes, costing from $25,000 to $250,000. They are generally physically smaller than mainframes and are usually housed in a single physical package. Minicomputers are usually slower and less powerful than mainframes, and while they support multiple users, they often support fewer of these than mainframes. Organizations may own several minicomputers, generally at the department level, and such computers are mainly found in an office environment with no or minimal special environmental conditioning. A very small special staff, if any, is provided.

C.5.2.4.3   Microcomputers

Microcomputers, often called micros, are relatively cheap, costing from less than $1,000 to about $25,000. They generally have a central processing unit on a single chip. Microcomputers are slower and less powerful than minicomputers and generally do not support multiple users. Such computers are usually available to individuals within departments with no special environmental or staff support.

C.5.2.4.3.1   Personal computers

Personal computers are microcomputers that are or could reasonably be owned by individuals for personal use.

C.5.2.4.3.2   Workstations

The term "workstation" is particularly ambiguous. One definition says that workstations are microcomputers owned by organizations and used by individuals. Usually, several employees will share a workstation, although sometimes it will have only a single user. In such cases, workstations overlap the personal computer definition. The use of the term is often associated with organizations that use microcomputers to prepare or manipulate data residing primarily in a mainframe or minicomputer and sometimes refers to a microcomputer used as a terminal for a minicomputer or mainframe. Often the term "workstation" is used by organizations when the term "personal computer" might lead to rejection of a purchase request.

A second meaning for the term "workstation" defines it as a fast, powerful, single-user computer that contains much RAM and often yields superior graphics capability. Advanced microcomputers used in artificial intelligence research, image processing, and scientific research are often called workstations.

C.5.2.4.3.3   Portable computers

Portable computers are microcomputers designed to be carried. They range from hand-held units through notebook-sized computers up to those machines that can best be described as transportable.

C.5.2.4.3.4   OEM suppliers

Microcomputers often are used in other devices like laser printers. When used as subassemblies, microcomputers are obtained from original equipment manufacturer (OEM) suppliers. Such units are then repackaged with the system assembler's name and resold.

C.5.2.5   Operation modes

Some computers are designed for operation by a single individual; others are suitable for many users. The way in which use is performed is defined in terms of mode of operation.

C.5.2.5.1   Batch (offline)

In batch operations, individual jobs are performed one after another in order of first come, first served. This was the computer's original mode of function and is still common in computers that serve many departments, especially those few computers that still use Hollerith cards.

Users under a batch system prepare instructions for the computer, then transmit them to the computer for processing. When their turn comes, the instructions and any necessary data are fed to the computer. When processing is completed, the user returns to the computer and obtains the output. (See figure 17.)

Such a mode of operation is frustrating in any case but especially when errors are detected since the user must correct the error and resubmit the job. In situations where users must interact with the computer, such as in word processing, batch mode is not a reasonable operations choice, although it has been attempted.

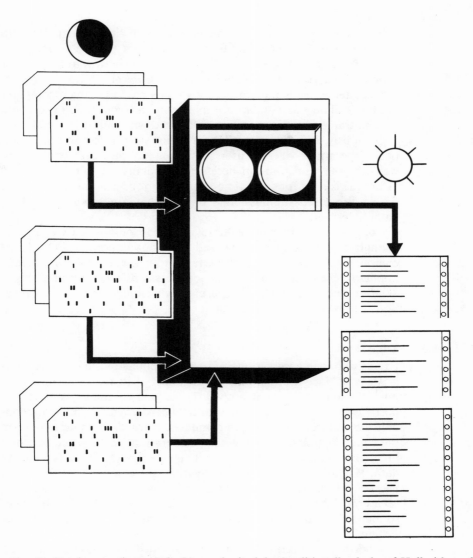

Fig. 17. Batch operations mode. User submits jobs (traditionally, decks of Hollerith cards) at end of work day for computer processing overnight (left); user picks up output the next morning (right).

While batch operation is not efficient for individual users, it does optimize computer usage. Therefore, it was the mode of choice when computers were scarce, expensive, and slow. It is still used today when no user intervention is required—for example, when processing a series of input files that have already been checked for errors.

129

C.5.2.5.2   Online

When there is a direct connection and therefore direct interaction with the computer, the user is said to be online. Such a mode of operation allows for data and operations corrections and changes to be made as soon as the need arises and allows the user to receive his or her results immediately. This is the normal operations mode for microcomputer use but is almost as standard for minicomputers and is quite common in mainframe use. A term often associated with online is "realtime."

Obviously, it would be possible for online systems to also be used for batch operations where a user submits a job via direct connection, waits for the results, and if necessary resubmits the job. This hybrid technique is used for some time-consuming jobs in some systems, but online also offers the possibility of immediate operation, something batch does not.

Computers operate in realtime when the output arrives quickly enough that the results can be used to modify operations. This is the computer equivalent to operating fast enough, and while this usually implies online operations, it does not necessarily require it in all cases. Where events in the real world occur slowly enough, even batch operations can be considered realtime.

C.5.2.5.3   Time sharing

Exclusive online access to mainframe computers by single individuals is wasteful since the computer spends most of its time waiting for input and to a lesser extent output. These long computer waits can be partly overcome through time sharing where several or many individuals are connected to a single computer. Normal computers perform only one function at a time. When an operation is completed, the computer checks the other users to see if anyone is ready to send or receive data. When it locates such an individual, the computer performs the necessary tasks then checks for the next user. While no one user receives the computer's sole attention, the mainframe computer operates so much faster than the remote user that it appears to be a single-user system.

When a mainframe's capacities are exceeded, this illusion of being a single-user system is shattered, and users wait for the computer to get around to them. The time it takes the computer to cycle around to the same user is called the response time. Response time is a sum of both processing time and input and output time. To reduce the input and output time, data to be input or output are sometimes stored in temporary memory locations called buffers. Rather than waiting for an entire document to print before handling the next job, a computer might write the document to a buffer then go on to the next task while the data move from the buffer to the printer.

A more generalized meaning of the term "response time" is the time from entering a command to the computer to the time the computer presents the results of that command. This definition, especially common with microcomputers, takes into account items such as disk access time and necessary processing.

C.5.2.5.4   Local area networks

Local area networks (LANs) can be considered another mode of computer operation, one that combines some of the best features of the online and time sharing modes. LANs are interconnections of computers and peripherals that allow optimal resource sharing. For example, printers connected to single microcomputers are often unused a large portion of the time; several microcomputers using a LAN could share a printer. In the same way, large hard disks, modems, and even mainframe computers can be used along with microcomputers as elements, often called nodes, in a local area network.

C.5.2.5.4.1 Network configurations

It is not sufficient to simply connect cables between various LAN units in a haphazard fashion. Over the years, several network configurations, or topologies, have evolved. The three most common are the star, ring, and backbone networks. In the star pattern, each node is connected to a central network server, often a minicomputer or mainframe, that mediates use of the system resources. (See figure 18.) In ring networks, the nodes are connected in a circular pattern with data being passed along the ring to the server. (See figure 19.) In the backbone, or bus, configuration, each node is connected to a single main cable (the backbone) by its own cable. In this configuration, the server controls which message is extracted from the bus for immediate processing. (See figure 20.)

C.5.2.5.4.2 Types of transmission technologies

Two main technologies are used in LANs: broadband transmission and baseband transmission. In broadband technology, the signals are effectively at radio frequencies, which is similar to cable television. Broadband transmission permits a single cable to carry several data channels but is complex and expensive. Baseband transmission requires more cables (one per channel) but is less complex and allows faster data transmission.

C.5.2.5.4.3 LAN protocols

The rules that ensure orderly use of LAN resources make up the protocol of the network. Three major types of protocol are used: polling, token passing, and CSMA/CD. In the polling protocol, the network server polls each node in turn to determine if it requires use of the network. If it does, that device is connected, and when it is finished with its job or a definite part of the job, the server polls the next node. If a

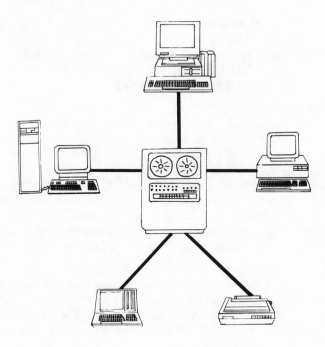

Fig. 18. Star network

node requires no action, the server immediately polls the next node. Thus, there is no possibility of two nodes simultaneously requesting use of the server's resources, but a significant amount of unproductive work, or overhead, is expended in polling disinterested nodes. Polling protocols are especially associated with star networks, although they can be implemented with other topologies.

The token passing protocol is generally implemented with ring networks. In such a scheme, a unique series of bits (the token) is passed from node to node around the ring. Only when a node possesses the token can it send or receive data. It does this by sending the data along with the name or address of the node to which the data are destined. As each node along the ring receives the token, it looks at the data's address to see if they are intended for it. If the data are not destined for that node, the node passes the token, address, and data along to the next node, which examines it. When a node possessing the token finds its own address along with data, it performs whatever function is called for (for example, printing or communication), formulates and addresses a response if necessary, and passes it along with the token. If no response is called for at that time, the bare token is passed, allowing the next node to take the token, attach an address and data, and pass it

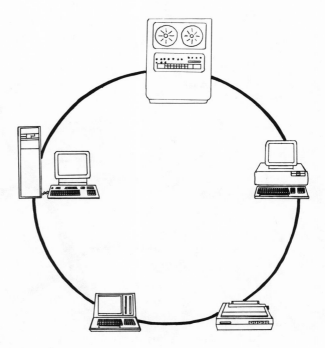

Fig. 19. Ring network

on. Only one node at a time can function under such a system, resulting in a highly disciplined network, although the function of passing
and examining the token by each node results in a large amount of
overhead.

The final major protocol, carrier-sense multiple access with colli-
sion detection (CSMA/CD), takes a much more brute force approach.
In this protocol, each node can try to access the server or another node
when it needs to, but the software keeps track of which node is using
the resources and will not allow any other node to access them until the
first is finished. Then the next node gains access and others are locked
out. Though it sounds chaotic, this system works well with much less
overhead than the token passing protocol. Of course, since human users generally work at much slower speeds than computers, the waiting
times in either system are often undetectable in practice.

C.5.2.6   Software
Software constitutes the instructions for the computer to execute.
Therefore, it is just as essential as the integrated circuits or other components of a computer since without instructions, the computer is
worthless. When computers are purchased, they usually come with

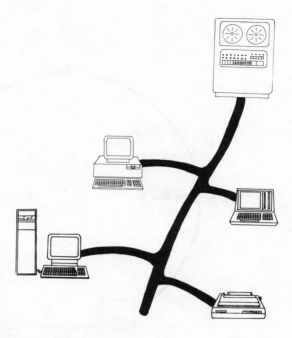

Fig. 20. Backbone, or bus, network

minimal software; the user is expected to purchase or write whatever is needed. Some computers are sold with software. This software is said to be bundled with the computer.

C.5.2.6.1   Operating systems

The most basic form of software is the operating system, which consists of the fundamental instructions that tell a computer how to input and output information, how to store and retrieve data and files, and how to interact with the user. Often microcomputers are supplied with both a simple operating system in ROM and a larger one on disk. This is necessary because the operating system is a fairly big program—certainly larger than ROM can easily accommodate. But without at least a few instructions in ROM, however, the computer could not retrieve the operating system from its storage location on the disk. The computer must thus pull itself up by its own bootstraps. This expression is the origin of the term "booting" the computer. When the system is booted, ROM sends sufficient instructions to read the first part of the disk file, which contains instructions on how to read the rest of the disk.

Since most operating systems for microcomputers today are distributed on disks, and since one of the operating system's main functions is to read disk files, the term "disk operating system" (DOS) has evolved. The same functions on larger systems are usually simply called operating systems.

Common disk operating systems for microcomputers include CP/M (used in many small personal computers in the past and one of the first operating systems developed), MS DOS (a refinement of CP/M used with larger systems), PC DOS (a proprietary system based on CP/M and nearly identical with MS DOS developed for IBM computers), and AppleDOS and PRODOS (used on many Apple computers). Minicomputers and mainframes generally use operating systems supplied by their manufacturers, although several third-party operating systems such as UNIX, and many special purpose operating systems such as the Pick operating system used by several turnkey library systems are available.

C.5.2.6.2   Languages

Computer languages are the means by which users control their computers. Employing computer languages, users may give the computer instructions that are optimal for the users' needs. It is not necessary for end-users today to know a computer language because many useful programs are available; however, those who do can often customize their software.

A computer itself deals only with binary codes, the 1s and 0s discussed in section C.5.2.2, while a human speaks various languages. Computer languages are artificial sets of terms that are more or less understandable to humans but that can be converted by the machine to its binary needs. Programs that translate these terms are called compilers if they deal with an entire program or interpreters if they work with a single instruction or line at a time.

Several levels of programs are generally acknowledged: machine language, assembly language, and various higher-level languages. Machine language programs are those produced in the computer's own 0 and 1 code and are almost never written by end-users, although professional programmers do sometimes use machine language when they need increased speed and reduced program space. When a machine takes a higher-level language and converts it to machine code, that is, compiles it, the code produced, while it works, is less than optimal. (See figures 21a and 21b.)

Higher-level languages such as BASIC, FORTRAN, COBOL, Pascal and PROLOG are much slower than machine languages because the computer must translate them into machine code before executing them, and the resulting machine code is seldom as efficient as if it had been written as machine-level code in the first place. There are many higher-level languages available because some problems, such as scien-

```
1110 1011 0100 1001 1001 0000 0100 0101      EB499045
0110 0100 0111 0100 0110 0101 0111 0010      64746572
0010 0000 0110 0110 0110 1001 0111 0010      20666972
0111 0011 0111 0100 0010 0000 0110 0100      73742064
0110 1001 0110 0111 0110 1001 0111 0100      69676974
0010 0000 0111 0100 0110 1111 0010 0000      20746F20
0110 0001 0110 0100 0110 0100 0011 1010      6164643A
0010 0000 0010 0100 0100 0101 0110 1110      2024456E
0111 0100 0110 0101 0111 0010 0010 0000      74657220
0111 0011 0110 0101 0110 0011 0110 1111      7365636F
0110 1110 0110 0100 0010 0000 0110 0100      6E642064
0110 1001 0110 0111 0110 1001 0111 0100      69676974
0000 0000 0000 0000 0000 0000 1000 1101      0000008D
0001 0110 0000 0011 0000 0001 1011 0100      16 0301B4
0000 1001 1100 1101 0010 0001 1011 0010      09CD21B2
0000 0001 1100 1101 0010 0001 0010 1100      01CD212C
0011 0000 1010 0010 0100 0110 0000 0001      30A24601
1011 0010 0000 1101 1011 0100 0000 0010      B20DB402
0000 0001 1011 0010 0000 1101 1011 0100      01B20DB4
0000 0010 1100 1101 0010 0001 1011 0010      02CD21B2
0000 1010 1011 0100 0000 0010 1100 1101      0AB402CD
0010 0001 1010 0000 0100 0110 0000 0001      21A04601
0000 0010 0000 0110 0100 0111 0000 0001      02064701
1010 0010 0100 1000 0000 0001 1011 0100      A24801B4
0000 0000 1010 0000 0100 1000 0000 0001      00A04801
1011 0010 0000 1010 1111 0110 1111 0010      B20AF6F2
1010 0010 0100 1001 0000 0001 1000 1000      A2490188
0010 0110 0100 1010 0000 0001 1000 1101      264A018D
0001 0110 0011 1010 0000 0001 1011 0100      163A01B4
0000 1001 1100 1101 0010 0001 1000 1010      09CD218A
0001 0110 0100 1001 0000 0001 1000 0000      16490180
1100 0010 0011 0000 1011 0100 0000 0010      C230B402
1100 1101 0010 0001 1000 1010 0001 0110      CD218A16
0100 1010 0000 0001 1000 0000 1100 0010      4A0180C2
0011 0000 1011 0100 0000 0010 1100 1101      30B402CD
0010 0001 1100 0011 0000 0000 0000 0000      21C30000
```

(a) (b)

Fig. 21. Computer programs. (a) Machine-language program; (b) Hexadecimal notation

tific, business, and artificial intelligence problems, are best dealt with by specialized languages. (See figure 21c.)

A compromise between high-level languages designed for humans and machine language is provided by assembly language. This language replaces machine language instructions with symbolic instructions used in a one-to-one correspondence with machine instructions. While assembler programs are not quite as fast as machine code programs, they are almost as fast; and while they are not as easily understood by humans as higher-level languages, they are still fairly easy to learn. Many applications programs are written in assembly language. (See figure 21d.)

Generally, lower-level languages are more machine dependent than higher-level ones. Each computer has its own machine codes, but a higher-level language such as BASIC is usually quite similar for differ-

```
program add;
var
   num1,num2: integer;
begin
   write('Enter first number to add: ');
   readln(num1);
   write('Enter second number to add: ');
   readln(num2);
   write('The sum is ',num1+num2);
end.
```

Fig. 21. (c) Higher-level language (Pascal)

ent machines. Also, because a single instruction in a higher-level language is translated into several machine language instructions, higher-level programs tend to need far fewer lines to accomplish the same tasks.

C.5.2.6.3 Utilities

Utilities are programs that help operating systems perform their functions. They are similar to operating systems in that their function is general but are similar to applications programs in that they are not necessary for operation. Typical utilities include programs that sort, ease communications, or deal with filing and storage of data. The compilers and interpreters discussed in the preceding section may be considered special forms of utility.

C.5.2.6.4 Applications

Computers exist to run applications programs. Other sorts of programs, including operating systems, utilities, and languages, exist only to create and use applications programs. Libraries use special purpose applications software to create computer catalogs, keep track of serials check-in, circulate materials, and perform other functions. Libraries also use applications programs of more general types. Probably the most common applications software programs are word processors, database management programs (which store and retrieve data), communications programs (for sharing data among users and computers), graphics programs (which create attractive and useful pictures and charts), games programs, and fiscal management packages, including spreadsheet and bookkeeping programs. (Spreadsheets are electronic versions of the columnar pads used as worksheets for budgeting, etc. Spreadsheet programs allow the user to establish relationships among the various items recorded and change all the recorded data in accordance with these relationships.)

```
ENTRY:    JMP       START
ASK1      DB        'Enter first digit to add: $'
ASK2      DB        'Enter second digit to add: $'
ANS       DB        'The sum is $'
NUM1      DB        ?
NUM2      DB        ?
SUM       DB        ?
TENS      DB        ?
ONES      DB        ?
START:    LEA       DX,ASK1
          MOV       AH,9
          INT       21H
          MOV       AH,1
          INT       21H
          SUB       AL,30H
          MOV       NUM1,AL
          MOV       DL,0DH
          MOV       AH,2
          INT       21H
          MOV       DL,0AH
          MOV       AH,2
          INT       21H
          LEA       DX,ASK2
          MOV       AH,9
          INT       21H
          MOV       AH,1
          INT       21H
          SUB       AL,30H
          MOV       NUM2,AL
          MOV       DL,0DH
          MOV       AH,2
          INT       21H
          MOV       DL,0AH
          MOV       AH,2
          INT       21H
          MOV       AL,NUM1
          ADD       AL,NUM2
          MOV       SUM,AL
          MOV       AH,0
          MOV       AL,SUM
          MOV       DL,10D
          DIV       DL
          MOV       TENS,AL
          MOV       ONES,AH
          LEA       DX,ANS
          MOV       AH,9
          INT       21H
          MOV       DL,TENS
          ADD       DL,30H
          MOV       AH,2
          INT       21H
          MOV       DL,ONES
          ADD       DL,30H
          MOV       AH,2
          INT       21H
          RET
```

Fig. 21. (d) Assembly language

In addition to these major types of applications programs, there are a multitude of highly specialized programs to accomplish specific tasks. For example, some programs analyze geological samples, predict movement of heavenly bodies, and create and store genealogical tables. Users purchase or write applications software according to their needs.

C.5.2.7 Library applications

Libraries make use of general purpose programs, but they also use specialized programs of little interest outside the library and information science field. In some cases, libraries develop these applications themselves for use in their own facilities (in-house development); in other cases, they save time and money by purchasing programs that meet their needs or they make use of automated services provided by a network, consortium, or vendor.

C.5.2.7.1 Single-library uses

Applications programs presently available could enhance virtually every phase of library operation. There are accounting and reporting packages for management, acquisitions programs, circulation programs, interlibrary loan programs, special purpose database management programs for reference use, cataloging programs, and public catalog programs that make use of the records the cataloging programs produce.

C.5.2.7.1.1 Integrated systems

Libraries that use a variety of individual programs, or modules, often find that they have difficulty getting the programs to work together and that many files and programs used in each application are duplicated—an inefficient and costly situation. Such problems with single-purpose systems are now being overcome through use of integrated systems—programs that deal with library operations as a whole or with large portions of library operations. These programs use modules that create and access single files for various operations. Integrated systems are thus more efficient than the individual programs they replace, although they are also more vulnerable to defects that render the entire integrated system inoperable rather than only a single module. (See figures 22 and 23.)

Both single-purpose and integrated systems may be written in-house or purchased from commercial vendors. The tradeoff is between system cost (commercial systems' development costs are often shared by many users) and system personalization (commercial systems must match the general needs of a great number of users; therefore, they generally don't match exactly the specific needs of any single user). Some library systems are advertised as being turnkey systems; that is, they may be installed on a library's computer, and when the computer

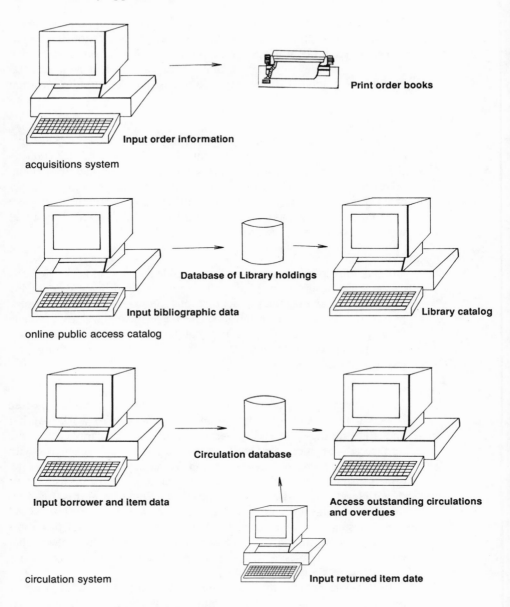

Print order books

Input order information

acquisitions system

Database of Library holdings

Input bibliographic data

Library catalog

online public access catalog

Circulation database

Input borrower and item data

Access outstanding circulations and overdues

circulation system

Input returned item date

Fig. 22. Three single-purpose systems

is turned on, the systems are ready to operate. Experience has shown that turnkey systems require varying amounts of special tweaking to make them operate at specific locations, although some do approach actual turnkey status.

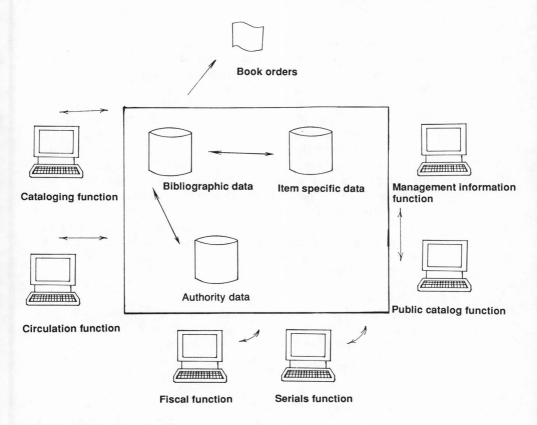

Book orders

Cataloging function

Bibliographic data

Item specific data

Management information function

Circulation function

Authority data

Public catalog function

Fiscal function

Serials function

Fig. 23. An integrated system

C.5.2.7.2   Multilibrary uses

Some computer applications, such as circulation, are best controlled at the local level. Others, because of the value of shared data or the ability to amortize costs over a larger base, are more efficient when several libraries cooperate. Some of the more common multilibrary applications are given below.

C.5.2.7.2.1   Operational support networks

Operational support networks, often called bibliographic utilities, provide assistance for the member libraries' day-to-day operations. Examples of these networks include the Online Computer Library Center (OCLC), the Western Library Network (WLN), and various regional library networks. Typical services supplied by operational support networks include provision of cataloging records, interlibrary loan communications, and various printing and production services.

C.5.2.7.2.2   Bibliographic citation networks

Bibliographic citation networks are generally used for reference. They include such well-known vendors as DIALOG and BRS, which obtain databases of bibliographic citations and then make them available using a basically standard search language. Because in the past few individual libraries could afford to purchase databases or bear the cost of the database management programs necessary for their use, citation networks made good economic sense. Recently, databases have been distributed on optical digital disks. These disks allow individual libraries to maintain and access the most often used databases locally, but will probably not affect the provision of more esoteric databases.

Recently, citation networks have made the entire text of documents available to their members. Such materials can be provided by mail, by telefacsimile, or by downloading the document to a library's computer. While cost and speed are still limiting factors, these services are attractive for out-of-print materials and for articles appearing in journals not locally available.

C.5.2.7.2.3   Nonbibliographic uses

A third kind of multiple-library application is the provision of nonbibliographic data. These services, often offered by the same companies that supply bibliographic data, allow access to numerical data such as census and stock market reports, to electronic mail and teleconferencing facilities, to travel and banking agencies, and to many other special-purpose facilities. Such applications may be intended primarily for libraries, like the services provided by traditional library vendors, or libraries may be just one class of user accessing the network, as when libraries communicate with public systems such as Compuserve or The Source.

C.6   Transportation

Books are heavy. This simple fact results in transportation problems that are often unappreciated.

C.6.1   External

Transportation outside the library building falls into two main categories: delivering materials and services directly to patrons through bookmobiles and transporting materials between libraries or branches through delivery vehicles.

C.6.1.1   Bookmobiles

Bookmobiles, or mobile libraries as they are called in the United Kingdom, have a long history. Their roots are planted in at least the late nineteenth century, and motorized vehicles were in use during the second decade of the present century. Nonetheless, these vehicles became common only when a national commitment to rural library services was made during the postwar era and specifically when this commitment was given financial credibility through the Library Services Act and later the Library Services and Construction Act.

The financial aid allowed a large number of libraries to purchase bookmobiles, and this customer base led to specialized manufacturers, especially the Gerstenslager Company and the Thomas F. Moroney Company. While the increasing cost of vehicle fuel and the reduction in federal aid has resulted in this market greatly decreasing, many of the machines purchased with LSCA money are still on the road.

C.6.1.1.1   Types of vehicles

Bookmobiles can be divided into self-powered and trailer types. Self-powered vehicles vary from converted recreational vehicles based on $3/4$-ton chassis to 10-ton specially produced trucks. Trailers vary within the same range, from the lightest units towed behind automobiles or pickup trucks to elaborate semimobile branches developed from mobile homes.

C.6.1.1.2   Bookmobile equipment

All bookmobiles must have facilities for storing materials and for circulating them. Generally, they also have some access to electrical power. In its simplest form, this electricity may be 12 volts derived directly from the vehicle's own electrical system, but generally, electricity is either locally generated or obtained by taps on commercial power. The 12-volt option is only marginally useful since operation of lights or book-charging machines soon depletes the vehicle's battery. Generators are commonly used when a bookmobile makes many stops or operates at remote locations where commercial electricity is not available.

Virtually all equipment found in libraries has been adapted for and operated in bookmobiles, including charging apparatus, microform readers, video and film projectors, and computers. Voice and data contact with main libraries can be established using telephone facilities or radio (see C.2).

C.6.1.2   Delivery vehicles

The main requirements for library delivery vehicles is that they have easy access and sufficient load-carrying capacity. Quarter-ton vehicles generally are insufficient for library service, and care must be taken to avoid overloading $3/4$-ton vehicles.

Some form of load retention is also necessary, either by using sloping side-mounted shelves such as those commonly found in bookmobiles or by using passenger protection grills. Without such devices, a vehicle's sudden stop could yield potentially tragic results.

Finally, libraries with small delivery quantities often find that using commercial services is less expensive than purchasing and maintaining their own vehicles.

C.6.2   Internal

Within libraries, large numbers of books must be moved from technical service areas to the shelves, from circulation to the shelves, and when relocating parts of the collection.

C.6.2.1   Booktrucks

Booktrucks are the most common device for moving quantities of books within a library. They commonly have two or three shelves and are made of metal or wood.

Once again, a major concern is the booktruck's load-handling capability. Because a heavily loaded booktruck can easily weigh more than 500 pounds, libraries must purchase robust units. In addition to load capacity, desirable characteristics include a low center of gravity and large wide wheels. Note that these two characteristics are interactive, and the best tradeoff between wheel size and center of gravity must be determined in each library.

While booktrucks might be considered low-tech items, there are a number of vehicle options available, including special wheels for outdoor use, rubber bumpers, and provision for displaying books as well as transporting magazines or other special media.

C.6.2.2   Elevators

Obviously, booktrucks cannot move books between floors. For vertical movement, elevators are a necessity. Probably the only aspect of an elevator that might prove useful to librarians is its safe loading factor An elevator that can safely hold eighteen persons might be overtaxed by six or seven booktrucks. Dumbwaiter elevators that hold only one or two booktrucks are generally not suitable for library use.

C.7   Patron-use equipment

For the most part, all equipment discussed so far has been for use by library staff. Although there are exceptions (patrons often use library copiers), libraries hardly expect patrons to borrow bookmobiles or use the circulation system's minicomputer. There are devices, however, that are frequently used by patrons, often more than by librarians. Such devices are commonly divided into microform and audiovisual equipment.

C.7.1   Microforms

Microforms are reproductions, generally by photographic techniques, in a form much smaller than the original (see B.1.5.2). This reproduction is obviously useful when size reduction is necessary, as when backfiles of newspapers must be maintained for reference use, but it is also useful when the original is rare or fragile. Materials are usually reduced ten to forty times; therefore, magnifications of equal amounts are necessary for use. Less common are the ultraforms that have been reduced over ninety times and can even exceed (in a very few cases) 200 times. Each format may be positive (dark characters on a clear background) or negative (clear characters on a dark background). Color film, although expensive, is sometimes used when color reproduction is important.

C.7.1.1   By format

There are several types of microforms; some are viewed by transmission of light (microfiche and microfilm) and others by reflection (microopaques).

C.7.1.1.1   Film

Microfilm images are arranged serially along a single strip of film. The film is wound on a reel. To locate an image, the frames preceding it must be wound onto a takeup reel. Film is a serial storage medium analogous to magnetic tape.

Microfilm is available in 16- and 35-millimeter formats, in positive and negative reproduction, and in color and black and white.

C.7.1.1.2   Fiche

In microfiche, an original document's individual pages are reproduced in serial form across a single sheet of film. Each of these images is called a frame. The word "fiche" itself is French for "card," and the film sheets are, indeed, index card sized—4 by 6 (or more rarely 3 by 5) inches or their metric equivalents. Microfiche is more easily accessed than microfilm but also is more easily misfiled or lost.

Viewers operate by placing the fiche under a cover sheet of glass, shining light through the fiche and glass, collecting and focusing this light through lenses, and then projecting the resulting image onto a mat surface rear-projection screen. (See figure 24a.) In microfiche viewers, the fiche and cover glass are movable, and individual frames on the fiche may be directly accessed. (See figure 24b.)

C.7.1.1.3   Opaque

Microopaque items are almost obsolete, but libraries still have them in their collections, and therefore librarians must be familiar with them. Microopaques are generally 3 by 5 inches or 6.5 by 8.5 inches and are viewed by reflecting light off the card, gathering the light with mirrors, focusing it, and then projecting it as for film and fiche. While several companies have made efforts to use microopaques for library materials (for example, Readex, later named Newsbank, reissued many hard-to-find scholarly works in this format), the format was limited by

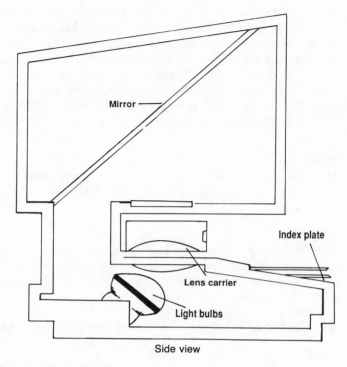

Fig. 24. A typical microfiche reader.

specialized equipment, was difficult to reproduce, and is largely of historical interest.

C.7.1.2   By use

Libraries seldom circulate their microforms. The special equipment used to view them, their physical delicacy, and the difficulties of replacing damaged items generally require that they be used on-site or that a special reader/printer be used to enlarge the material and produce copies. Two modes of microform use may be cited: reading and printing.

C.7.1.2.1   Reading

Microforms are of little use unless they are enlarged. Using microform readers, patrons or librarians may read the information recorded in microform and take notes. This is sometimes sufficient for research.

C.7.1.2.2   Printing

Even if libraries were willing to lend microforms, patrons seldom have microform readers at home. Therefore, libraries almost have to own reader/printers. These printers are similar to chemical nonxerographic copiers and work on a photographic principle. Light is reflected off or

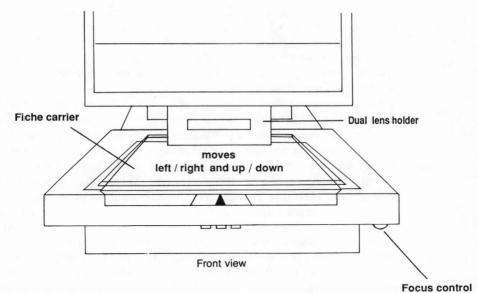

Fiche carrier

moves
left / right and up / down

Dual lens holder

Front view

Focus control

Fig. 24. *Continued*

transmitted through the microform, modifying the chemical structure of sensitized paper, which, after suitable development, is delivered to users needing enlarged paper copies of microforms for extended research.

C.7.2   AV equipment

Audiovisual (AV) material refers to the mass of library materials that are neither printed materials nor microforms of such materials (see B.1.5). The term covers a wide variety of media and formats, all of which share the common characteristics of requiring hardware for their use.

C.7.2.1   Sound

Sound, or audio, materials may be magnetically, optically, or structurally recorded. Magnetic recordings are on tapes of various sorts; optical recordings are mostly CD-ROM recordings; and structural recordings include the various versions of sound disks.

C.7.2.1.1   Sound disks

Sound disks record sound by creating gross physical variations in the topography of grooves making up the recording. Such variations in surface are detected by mechanical motion detectors of various sorts (crystal, ceramic, or magnetic) and are converted into loudness and pitch variations corresponding to the depth and closeness of the variations.

147

C.7.2.1.2   *Sound tape*

Sound disks are available in several formats and recording speeds, the most common being 33¹/₃ and 45 revolutions per minute (rpm). Some older library collections also contain recordings made at 78 rpm, and some talking books and archival transcriptions are available at 16 rpm. Generally speaking, the 33¹/₃ rpm disk with grooves .001 inch wide is the form most common in libraries.

Most such recordings are produced in stereophonic (two-channel) formats, but many single-channel (monaural) recordings were made and are commonly available in libraries. In stereo recordings, two microphones are used to record opposite sides of the grooves. When these are played back, obviously through separate amplifiers and speakers, the same separation of sounds present when the recording was made is reproduced. Therefore, two-channel stereo recordings present a much more realistic representation of the original sound than monophonic recordings. Carrying this concept to its next level, four-channel (quadraphonic) recordings were made, but despite heavy promotion, the benefits could not overcome the great number of already installed stereo units, and the quadraphonic format is seldom encountered today.

Sound disks are subject to severe degradation of sound as their surfaces become abraded through use. While the reproduction quality and signal-to-noise ratio of virgin disks may surpass that of other media, this high quality is seldom maintained. However, against this disadvantage libraries weigh the sound disk's ease of use. Most library patrons already own a stereo phonograph, and therefore the sound disk remains a useful medium.

C.7.2.1.2   Sound tape

While the sound disk is a direct-access medium, tape is serial: individual selections are recorded one after the other on a strip of tape. This tape is produced by adhering a thin layer of magnetic material to a base of acetate, polyester, or mylar. Sound tape is available in both reel-to-reel and cassette formats with reel-to-reel tapes ordinarily being ¹/₄-inch wide and cassettes ¹/₈-inch wide. There is also a less common ¹/₄-inch enclosed format called a tape cartridge. In any case, the tape may be of various thicknesses, ranging from .5 mil (a thousandth of an inch) to 1.5 mil with thinner tape providing longer playing times for a given wound diameter at the expense of increased stretching, breaking problems, and danger of interference between adjacent layers of tape, called print-through.

Another variable in tape format is recording speed. Speeds of from 1⁷/₈ inches per second (ips) to 15 ips are most common with the higher speeds and wider tape formats producing better reproduction at higher cost. The most common speeds for reel-to-reel recorders are

148

$3^3/_4$ and $7^1/_2$ ips, and $1^7/_8$ ips for cassette machines. Tapes recorded at a given speed must be played back at the same speed.

In a magnetic tape's unrecorded state, the small particles that make up its coating are distributed randomly. Recording orders these particles in terms of both intensity and density in a way that corresponds to the loudness and pitch of the original sound. Reproduction uses electronic means to sense these orderly variations in magnetic structure and turn them back into sound.

As in disk recordings, tapes may be stereo or monaural. But unlike disks, tapes can be reused, or recorded over. This characteristic is a constant problem for libraries, although it is partly alleviated in cassettes by a record protect tab. This tab is a small piece of plastic present in new tapes that can be removed after recording. In most tape recorders, a microswitch is placed so as to detect the presence or absence of this tab. When no tab is present, the machine will not record, thus protecting the tape against accidental rerecording. Of course, since tapes are recorded magnetically, magnetic fields can alter or erase the recording; therefore, libraries should not store tapes near devices that might produce magnetic fields, such as transformers and television sets.

Despite these dangers, tapes are less prone to quality degradation than disks and therefore make an attractive alternative to disks in library collections.

C.7.2.1.3   Compact sound disks

A medium of increasing importance to libraries is the compact sound disk, often shortened to just compact disk or CD. Because this system uses digital techniques to record audio information, they are also called digital disks. CDs are attractive to libraries because, while their unit cost is higher than that of cassettes or sound disks, they are capable of reproducing better sound and are much less susceptible to the distortion responsible for extraneous noise in the other sound media. In fact, a well-engineered compact disk contains no audible distortion and none of the wow, rumble, flutter, or crosstalk associated with tape or phonograph reproduction. Another advantage of CDs is that while they are smaller than standard disks (4.72 inches or 12 centimeters), they play longer (about 75 minutes for CDs versus about 50 minutes for $33^1/_3$ rpm records), although CD musical recordings often do not take full advantage of this longer playing time.

To record CD disks, the fluctuating analog audio signal is converted to digital form by a technique known as sampling. This technique monitors the signal 44,100 times each second and records each value. These data are recorded in much the same way computer data are recorded, using 16-bit "words." These words are then used to modulate a laser that burns 1-micrometer pits onto the surface of the disk. These pits form a spiral pattern with adjacent lines of pits being about 1.6 micrometers apart. The unpitted area between pits is called a land. Once a disk has been recorded, it is coated with a clear plastic layer to protect the surface.

Playback occurs when the light from a laser in the player reflects off the disk's surface. The reflected light varies in intensity with the presence or absence of pits, that is, with each transition from land to pit or pit to land. This light is detected by a photodetector that produces an electrical signal that varies in time with the light variation. This signal is then converted back into an analog signal, amplified, and reproduced. (See figure 25.)

In addition to the basic digital/analog difference, there are several factors that make CD recordings unique. For example, the recording and therefore the playback moves from the inside of the disk outward rather than from the edge toward the center. Also different from phonograph disks is the direction of rotation: CDs rotate counterclockwise. Finally, in order to maintain tight packing of data (pits and lands) at the outer edges, the disk's speed actually slows down as the laser moves out from the center; the disk begins at about 500 rpm and decreases to about 200 rpm.

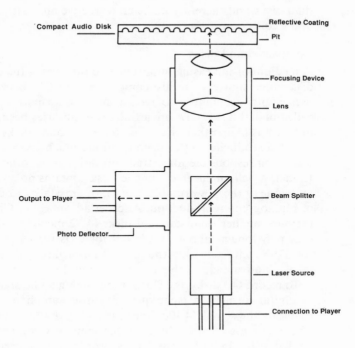

Fig. 25. Compact audio disk player

The above description has been simplified in the interest of intelligibility. In actuality, the audio signal is not recorded in a perfectly linear fashion; instead, parts of each sampling datum are stored at different places on the disk and then reassembled upon playback. This technique is responsible for much of the CD's immunity to noise. A scratch, for example, does not destroy the entire signal at any point because the signal is stored in several places. In addition, missing data can be reconstructed using computer techniques to fill in sound holes. In addition to recording sound, CDs can record other data such as television images. In fact, less than half of the data recorded on a compact disk are actual sound; the rest are overhead of various sorts. It is expected that some of this technology will be available for storing digitized images in the future.

C.7.2.2   Video

Video recordings are a relatively new medium for library collections. In theory, video recordings are similar to the audio recordings discussed above; however, the larger bandwidth and more critical tolerances involved make both the machines and the media more fragile. Nonetheless, libraries have been collecting video recordings for some years. The earliest format was reel-to-reel, but such material is rare now with most recordings collected in one of the common cassette formats.

The two most common cassette formats are the VHS and the Beta formats. While they use similar technology (both, for example, use 1/2-inch tape), the two are not interchangeable. Fortunately, most recordings are available in both formats. Currently, however, the VHS format enjoys a clear lead in number of tapes available and in cost and is generally more common. If a library owns both types of machines, one format can be converted to the other by connecting the output of the machine with the undesired format to the input of the machine with the desired format and creating, or dubbing, a new copy.

C.7.2.3   Film

Films, or motion pictures, have long been a part of library collections. In this medium, a series of photographs (similar to slides in that they are positive nonopaque images) are exposed. These images are produced at a constant pace by matching film advance with shutter opening rates. When projected at an equal rate, because of the smoothing effect of the brain's persistence of vision, the images reproduce the motion of the original.

The main variable in films is their width; 35 millimeter film is common for commercial projection, 16mm is popular for library use, and 8mm and its cousin super-8 is common for home use. Some formats also have several possible speeds, expressed in terms of frames projected per second (fps).

While the hardware necessary for reproduction is in some ways more delicate than that for video cassettes, and while far fewer patrons own 16mm motion picture projectors, films are common in libraries both because collections were begun before video became available and because many classic motion pictures have not been and may never be converted to video formats.

C.7.2.4   Other

Other patron-use equipment owned by libraries may include slide projectors, filmstrip viewers and projectors, and microcomputers. Virtually all other media and devices—from the common 2-by-2 inch transparency, to oscilloscopes, to dress patterns, to dwell meters—have been obtained by libraries. Before purchasing any item, libraries are advised to determine its likely use, its maintenance and repair needs, and its cost.

C.8   Miscellaneous

Usually a miscellaneous section in any discussion is an admission of defeat. Certainly it is in this case: it represents those items the taxonomy fails to cover.

C.8.1   Book-marking equipment

Books must be marked with their call numbers (see B.3.4.1) in order to be shelved and retrieved. Various methods have been used for marking: labels glued and lacquered on, India ink, temperature-set inks, and mechanical means. Only the last two involve technology to any great extent, and therefore only these will be discussed here.

Permanence is of great importance in marking books. One technique used to achieve permanence is heat transfer. In this system, a meltable substance is applied using a pointed electrically heated stylus that resembles a soldering iron. The material for transfer is supplied on a plastic substrate, that is, as coated sheets of plastic. The stylus is heated and the book's call number is written freehand using the hot stylus with the sheet of plastic covered with the meltable "ink" interposed between the book and the pen. This technique, while producing a long-lasting and legible call number, is dependent on the artistic and lettering ability of the person applying the letters and numbers. Such ability varies from person to person.

As a means of improving upon freehand lettering, Batelle Memorial Institute developed a system that allows a label produced by a typewriter or a computer printer to be permanently bonded to a book's spine. In this system, developed in the 1960s, a typewriter using a special platen produces a label on a special plastic tape that is coated with a heat bonding glue. This label, available in several widths, is then automatically covered with a clear plastic tape that keeps it from smearing. This sandwich of tapes is trimmed to the correct length and affixed to the book's spine. A special iron is then heated to the proper temperature and applied to the label, melting the glue and firmly attaching the label to the book. This system, sold by Gaylord Brothers, is the current standard for labeling book spines.

C.8.2   **Noncomputerized circulation systems**

While circulation systems for new libraries are likely to be computer-based, older libraries often still use noncomputerized systems unless they were recently converted to the newer technology. Several of the more common mechanized systems are listed below.

C.8.2.1   Photographic

In photographic systems, a patron's borrower's card, which may be a driver's license or other document, is photographed along with a book card or the title page of the book to be borrowed and a consecutively numbered transaction card. Numbers on the transaction cards are duplicates of numbers appearing on transaction sheets. The transaction card is then inserted into a pocket glued inside the book's cover. Reels of film representing the circulation for a period are processed and returned to the library.

When the book is returned, the transaction card is removed and its number crossed off the transaction sheet. Overdue books are represented by numbers not crossed off these sheets. These numbers are then found on the returned rolls of film, a task made simpler by the fact that the images on the film are in the same consecutive order as the numbers on the transaction sheet.

Systems of this type were once used in libraries across the country, including large libraries. However, cost of materials, difficulties with unreadable photographs, and inefficiency of searching for materials in the reels of film have greatly reduced these systems' use.

C.8.2.2   Edge-notched cards

Edge-notched card (see C.4.2) charging systems, the most common of which is the McBee Keysort system, are among the most nearly automated of manual circulation systems. In this and similar systems, the due date is recorded using edge-notched cards while the bibliographic data are typed by the library or handwritten by the patron.

When a book circulates, the card is filed by due date but is still accessible by other data with which it is encoded, such as call or accession number. Thus, the date a book is due to be returned can be ascertained by needling the call numbers in the file of cards representing books checked out.

As a variation, such cards can be used as transaction cards in the photographic system described in the preceding section. Here the consecutively numbered and coded keysort cards for a given circulation period are searched for when their due date is passed. These cards represent transactions that have not been cleared and therefore that require overdue notices.

While the edge-notched card was a practicable technique for searching before the advent of the computer, the primary use for such cards now is in restocking current operations.

C.8.2.3   Newark/Gaylord

The Newark/Gaylord system and its variations are probably the most common book-charging systems. They are based on a book card that is prepared as a step in processing new books. This card usually records a book's author, title, call number, and sometimes its accession number. It is stored in a pocket glued to the back cover of each book. These pockets are marked with the same information as the book card. In the original nonmechanical system, borrowers wrote their names on the book cards, but in the Gaylord system, this is done mechanically.

Registered patrons are given cards with their names on them. They are also assigned unique borrower's numbers that are recorded in a book or more recently in a database. Also affixed to the borrower's card is a metal plate embossed with the borrower's number.

Circulation is accomplished by using a special machine that holds a small metal plate embossed with the due date. These plates must be changed daily and are available with and without years. When a book is to be charged, the library staff member takes the patron's card and inserts it into the charging machine along with the book card. The machine aligns the patron's number with the date due plate and positions both for printing by allowing the book card to sink against a notch in its edge. When they are properly aligned, a solenoid presses the date due and the patron ID number against an inked typewriter ribbon and then against the book card, recording both the patron number and the date due. At the same time, the edge of the book card is nibbled away by a special punch so that subsequent use will again properly align the card. The book cards can then be filed by due date and within this sequence by call number. The library employee then either stamps the date due on the book or inserts a previously dated card into the book pocket. (See figure 26.)

When the book is returned, the due date is checked, and the appropriate cards are searched. The book card is retrieved, replaces the date due card in the book's pocket (if such a card is used), and the book is ready to be shelved. Book cards still in the file after closing for a given day's date represent overdue books.

Refinements on this system, which represent tradeoffs against simplicity and ease of check-in, include filing cards by call number rather than date and using multiple book cards to allow retrieval by several keys.

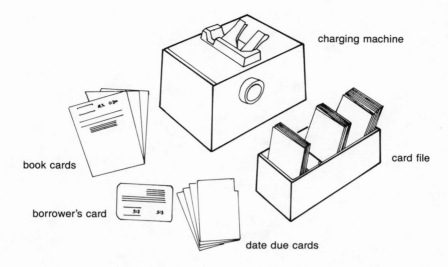

Fig. 26. Gaylord circulation system. The book cards have call number, author, title, and space for date due. The borrower's card has a metal identification number plate. The notch in the date due cards is to position the card in the charging machine. The file of cards is arranged in due-date order.

INDEX

157

Index

Index

Index

Mary Ellen Soper is an assistant professor in the Graduate School of Library and Information Science at the University of Washington, Seattle. She is the author of several articles that have appeared in such journals as *Reference Librarian* and has contributed a chapter to *Cataloging Special Materials* (Oryx Press, 1986). Soper is an active member of ALA, serving on several committees, including the committee on education for the Association for Library Collections and Technical Services and the committee on serials cataloging. Soper received both her master's and doctorate in library science from the University of Illinois, Urbana.

Larry N. Osborne is an associate professor in the Graduate School of Library Studies at the University of Hawaii at Manoa. He has published several articles on American academic libraries and has edited several issues of *Journal of Education for Library and Information Science*. Osborne received both his master's and doctorate in library science from the University of Pittsburgh. He was also a visiting scholar at Beijing Foreign Studies University in the People's Republic of China, and has taught extensively in Hong Kong.

Ronald R. Powell is an associate professor in the School of Library and Informational Science at the University of Missouri–Columbia. He is the author of *Basic Research Methods for Librarians,* second edition (Ablex Press, forthcoming). Powell is an active member of ALA and was listed in *Who's Who in Library and Information Services* (ALA, 1982). He received his doctorate in library science from the University of Illinois, Urbana.

Douglas L. Zweizig is a professor in the School of Library and Information Studies at the University of Wisconsin–Madison. He is a co-author of *Planning and Role Setting for Public Libraries: A Manual of Options and Procedures* and *Output Measures for Public Libraries: A Manual of Standardized Procedures,* second edition (ALA, 1987). Zweizig received his master's in library science from Rutgers University and his doctorate from Syracuse University.